BEFORE
YOU
MOVE

BEFORE
YOU
MOVE

A GUIDE TO
MAKING TRANSITIONS
IN MINISTRY

John R. Cionca

Kregel
Academic & Professional

Before You Move: A Guide to Making Transitions in Ministry

© 2004 by John R. Cionca

A revised and expanded edition of the previously published title *Red Light, Green Light: Discerning the Time for a Change in Ministry,* © 1994.

Published by Kregel Publications, a division of Kregel, Inc., P.O. Box 2607, Grand Rapids, MI 49501. Kregel Publications provides trusted, biblical publications for Christian growth and service.

Library of Congress Cataloging-in-Publication Data
Cionca, John R.
   Before you move: a guide to making transitions in ministry / by John R. Cionca.
      p. cm.
Includes bibliographical references.
   1. Clergy—Relocation. I. Title.
BV664.C558   2004
253'.2—dc22   2004011065

ISBN 0-8254-2392-9

Printed in the United States of America

1 2 3 4 5 / 08 07 06 05 04

To Aaron Cionca, my father,
and in memory of Anne Cionca, my mother,
who by example and counsel
have provided wise guidance.

CONTENTS

FIGURES

FOREWORD

AT LAST, A ROAD MAP FOR OUR bewildering journey through pastoral relations! John Cionca has written a most needful book for all who shepherd. It surprises me that we who pastor had to wait so long for such an insightful work. Now we have reasonable help as we ferret through our feelings on the subject of leaving or staying with our churches.

Monday-morning gloom is common to everyone who has ever pastored a church. Along the *a Gloria ad Nauseam* continuum, it is easy to feel that God loves us so much that He must surely wish for us a better situation. It has always been difficult to answer the skeptics' charge that God loves people too much to send them to hell. But in the case of pastors, why does He so often seem to want them there? Is all lost? No, occasionally in the midst of our ever-circling dyspepsia, the phone rings! It is the voice of God—*Gloria in Excelsis*—it's a pulpit committee! If it is a large church that is interested in us—glory! Even if it is a smaller church, it is at least another church—glory! Nonetheless, all is glory! Or is it?

Cionca has given us a guide that will help us untangle the circuitous logic of changing situations. It is often true that after the pastor/people honeymoon has ended, our *dearly beloved* have not been so *dear*. Nor have they been so able to see the genius of our leadership as they did on the Sunday we candidated. Should we stay and tough it out? After all, "godly sorrow brings repentance that leads to salvation" (2 Cor. 7:10). To fight or flee? That is the question.

I used to meet with two other ministers (fellow refugees from pain) for coffee every Monday morning. I liked those mornings when we three wallowed in our suffering as ministry-wounded brothers. We were all desperately busy souls. Our ultrabusy, oversized congregations saw to that. In fact, our churches barely gave us time to come down from our individual crosses to meet for breakfast. How often we spoke of the impossibility of holding our parish life and family life together. How often we dreamed aloud of walking off the job. Even more often, we fantasized about our retirement years, which seemed light-years away. We felt so hopeless.

Congregations have a way of eventually entangling us within a web of threads that bind our self-image to our emotions. Most of the time when I wanted to leave my church, it was because I was angry at the parishioners or hurt by them or disenchanted with them or bored with them—charges that all too often they also leveled at me. Cionca says that none of these is the best reason to move to another church because each implies an attitude of "I'll show them how hard it will be to find such a sterling saint for their next pastor." Cionca rehearses some splendid indicators that may be more worthy guides than the "I'll-show-them" syndrome. The author's red lights (signals of when *not* to change churches) are sensible and valid. Those red-light times can be seasons of pain. Nevertheless, says Cionca, there are tons of crises in leadership. Because leaving at such times would be a violation of pastoral ethics, the hurts of ministry alone should not mandate when we change situations. I used to say laughingly that the reason I stayed in my last parish for twenty-five years was that I could never get my crises and my pulpit calls in the same time frame. Often, when I hurt so badly that I would have gone *anywhere,* no search committee showed up. When things were mercifully happy, they came—but I had no need for them.

A key indicator in changing pulpits is timing; *timing is everything.* Cionca delivers a practical matrix of assessment in this workbook format. Often, through such considerations, a practical God tells us whether we are wise or unwise to consider moving. This book provides some checklists and other graphics that help you visually assess your feelings and potential at a particular church. You can even *graph* your woes more sensibly! The needs of pastors and congregations must fit together. This book discusses some of the important *fits* of congregational life. We should consider *Before You Move* as a kind of reference work for pastoral conscience. Above all, it will help us know if we are doing the right things for the right reasons.

In reading this book, I was struck by how inevitably preachers say, "God moved me to this church." But, in many evangelical churches, preachers change churches so often that they make God look indecisive or even shifty. A thumb-worn tale tells of a pastor who resigned by announcing, "This will be my last Sunday, for Jesus is calling me to another church" only to have the congregation rise and sing "What a Friend We Have in Jesus." Cionca makes it clear that pastors, too, might consider Jesus their friend if He called them elsewhere.

The emotional and spiritual reasons we make career decisions are difficult to assess. The practical reasons, however, deal quite sensibly with issues of church relationships. Pragmatic thinking can help us decide if we are being truly spiritual when we try to make spiritual decisions. Cionca's practical indicators can help us act *reasonably* when our emotional state is so frazzled that we cannot figure which end of the fight-or-flight argument we ought to choose. Don't buy this book to read philosophically. Instead, buy it to have it close at hand during the needy times of your life when you cannot decide if you would be better off to stay or to change churches. But beware! These days, pastoral disenchantment often amounts to a vast game of *pulpit roulette*. In the current world of two-year pastorates, you might be tempted to change for reasons that are almost entirely ego-defensive. Cionca thinks there is only one reason pastors should change churches—the call of God.

Read this book carefully, but never lend it. There may come a needy night when its wisdom will be for you the only light in a passage of darkness.

—CALVIN MILLER

PREFACE

FOR MORE THAN TWENTY YEARS, I have studied the field of pastoral transitions. Some of my gleanings have come from the writings of consultants and counselors, both within the church as well in the corporate world. However, most of my research has been conducted through interviews and observation, gathering insights via personal stories.

My personal journey in pastoral transition began after an eight-year season of fruitful ministry. A church in New Jersey contacted me regarding their need for a senior minister. My reply at that time was a cordial: "Thank you for your interest, but I'm quite happy in my present ministry." A few weeks later, however, the chairperson of the search committee followed up to see if I'd at least talk with them about their church. In response, I dictated a cassette tape that explained my reasons for wanting to remain where I was, yet indicating an openness if God were leading me elsewhere.

This dialog occurred during my eighth year of ministry at Trinity Church. Trinity was very special to us then and still is today. There in Mesa, Arizona, Barbara and I purchased our first home, experienced the birth of our two children, developed close friendships, and enjoyed a vibrant ministry. Part of me felt that we could serve happily there forever. But another part of me realized that giftedness and maturity might be moving us toward a fresh challenge.

Southwood Church updated Barbara and me every month or so

on the progress of its search for a new pastor. Over the course of a year, the pulpit committee had written a church profile, developed a pool of candidates, mailed letters of inquiry, visited six primary prospects, and conducted on-site interviews with two finalists.

Throughout this process, I had peace—that is, peace whenever the ball was in Southwood's court. My view of the sovereignty of God led me to believe that they would eliminate me if I were not the right person for their pastorate. On the other hand, when the ball was in my court—whether I would take the next step—an anxiety would surface. I honestly was willing to either go or stay, but I didn't know what was best. Why didn't God just zap me with some brilliant insight?

Rather than administering a divine zap, however, God used those seemingly long months to help me make significant observations and assessments. During that period of unsettledness, I considered my dreams for the kingdom, examined my giftedness, weighed family concerns, and sought counsel from friends. Although previous inquiries from churches had not led to a change, this one did. Several unmistakable green lights signaled a "go ahead" to proceed through this intersection of pastoral transition.

My experience is not unique. Hundreds of pastors recount similar stories of transition. For most of them, a critical and prolonged period of assessment preceded the decision to remain or move. Each of them indicated that the choice seemed to be a divine/human decision. They actively moved according to specific road signs, yet God also guided them through circumstances and the conveying of peace along the way.

The conclusion I've drawn from interviews with scores of colleagues across our country, and the foundational thesis of this book, is that God gives a pastor a double green light when a move is in order. The *green light of fitting* with a calling church and the *green light of freedom* to leave one's present ministry together signal that it's time to move. However, a red light from either a calling church or within one's present ministry will indicate the need to remain.

I first set forth these observations in my book *Red Light, Green Light: Discerning the Time for a Change in Ministry*. The volume now before you is a revision and expansion of that 1994 work.

The first two chapters of this book deal with presuppositions. We begin by identifying five red flags that can safeguard a minister from making a poor decision. Next, we consider the relationship of God's sovereignty to personal choice regarding call to ministry and subsequent transitions. Chapters 3 through 8 develop thirty-five guidelines for assessing a present ministry as well as an invitation to move. The material on pastoral evaluations (chapter 9) provides mirrors that reflect congregational values, and therefore are useful for determining how your ministry would fit with that church.

Chapters 10 through 12 consider three particular transitions: associate to senior minister, senior pastor to associate, and pastoral ministry to marketplace employment. The candidating process is detailed in chapter 13. "When You Want to Move, but No One's Knocking" (chapter 14) offers hope to colleagues who feel stuck. Chapter 15 advises the pastor on how to bring healthy closure to a ministry, regardless of the circumstances underlying the transition. "Jumping Out of the Blocks" (chapter 16) outlines a strategy for getting off to a good start in a new pastorate. And chapter 17 affirms ongoing kingdom service after the seasons of remunerated church ministry draw to a close.

No doubt, some people reading this book are hoping to sense God's leading. Others may be wondering what to say during a candidating interview or trying to figure out how to inform their congregation that they are leaving. Others are excited about moving from associate to senior pastor. Some feel as though the wind has been knocked out of their sails because they want to move, but no one is calling. Still others are feeling exhilarated, as they anticipate a blissful honeymoon with a new congregation. Each of us could share unique, yet similar, stories about church situations.

I wish that I could meet with each pastor who is considering a ministry change. The best I can do is pass on the observations and suggestions of colleagues who have learned and grown through transitions. This book is their collective advice. But, in addition to their wisdom and counsel, let's never forget Paul's encouraging affirmation that "he who began a good work in you will carry it on to completion until the day of Christ Jesus" (Phil. 1:6).

ACKNOWLEDGMENTS

FOR NEARLY TWO DECADES, I have studied pastoral transitions. Initially, my concern was personal: "Is it time for me to move?" Later, my perspective broadened as colleagues grappled with the same question. After each interview, lunch meeting, or ministerial meeting, I added a half-dozen 3 x 5 cards to an expanding "transitions" file that detailed stories, insights, warnings, and suggestions. Eventually, I began sharing the results at gatherings of denominational executives and also at seminars. Refinements by these practitioners resulted in a book titled *Red Light, Green Light: Discerning the Time for a Change in Ministry*. Now, ten years later, and with insights gained from two hundred additional consultations, this volume is a revised and expanded edition of that pastoral resource.

Before You Move: A Guide to Making Transitions in Ministry is not the work of a vocational-guidance guru. From its inception it has been a collaborative effort. To say that acknowledgments are appropriate is an understatement; therefore, I express deep appreciation to the following people:

Barbara, Ben, and Betsy: Fellow members of the Cionca family transition team

Dennis Newton Baker: Sagest of counselors

Bethel Seminary Administration: Encouragers of the project and providers of time for writing

Ministry Transitions Board Members: Friends and accountability
   partners
Gloria Metz: Lead computer wizard who transformed sound and
   scribble into attractive print
Dee Cawood: Finest editorial filter in the Southwest
Ministry colleagues: Insightful travelers committed to excellence
   in church service

1

THE MYTH OF THE
GREENER GRASS

Never open your mail on Mondays! That's the advice one pastor gives to those who are at the end of their parish rope. Questions of self-worth and ministry effectiveness can easily surface after an exhausting Sunday, especially in a situation where appreciation is rarely given. Monday morning dreams of "greener pastures" are not uncommon among ministerial colleagues.

In many situations, a change in pastors is beneficial for both the minister and the congregation. "Some pastors have taken their church as far as they can," acknowledged one district superintendent. "A change can offer [the pastor] a new challenge and allow their congregation to move into its next chapter under fresh leadership," acknowledged another. In fairness to our churches and ourselves, sometimes we need to move on.

Before we move too hastily, however, several words of caution are worth heeding. Those who have journeyed ahead of us have identified five "red flags" that warn us away from a premature move. So before reviewing particular signals for relocation, we should first consider the following presuppositions.

#1: Restlessness Alone Is Not a Reason to Move

Although restlessness is sometimes sovereignly aroused, more typically this feeling of unsettledness is situationally related. Personal time-tables and expectations, ministerial pressures, criticisms, family harmony, financial concerns, and life-cycle factors affect a pastor's sense of accomplishment. Yet, a search for fulfillment may prove misleading. For example, one pastor confided, "This is the first time since I've been in ministry that neither my parishioners nor I are growing. Maybe I'm not the person to take the church through the next chapter." Yet, after deeper consideration, he concluded that his restlessness was "primarily related to unrealistic expectations rather than an overall fit with the congregation." He decided to stay.

Several colleagues also related the importance of good health in sound decision making. "A lot of pastors are so out of shape physically that they couldn't make a good decision if they had to," observed one pastor. Another suggested, "Never make a decision when you're tired; better get rested and focused first."

Frustrations faced in one congregation may likewise surface elsewhere. Family tensions and financial concerns do not disappear through relocation. Mid-life issues will travel with us to another part of the country. And criticism will track down pastoral leaders wherever they settle. Therefore, before attributing restlessness to God's leading, honest self-examination is most appropriate.

#2: Perfect Congregations Do Not Exist

The challenges of pastoral ministry are enormous. More often than not, earthly rewards are not commensurate with energy expended. Ministers often endure criticism from the very people whom they are most eager to serve. Forced terminations are at a record high, which is perhaps why so many clergy conclude, "Who needs this? I'm out of here!"

When my family goes to McDonald's, Ben orders a quarter-pounder with cheese, Betsy the chicken McNuggets, Barbara a salad, and I take two regular burgers. If a family of four has different preferences on just a limited McDonald's menu, imagine the diversity and potential for disagreement in a congregation of a hundred, two hundred, or two thousand! What constitutes a good sermon? What type of music is best for worship? Who should make administrative decisions? How shall pastoral care be given? In a church of two hundred, you'll find two hundred different answers to such questions. You probably know all too well that perfect harmony doesn't exist in your congregation. But watch out! While diversity of opinion permeates your present church, it will also reside in the next one you shepherd.

When our dreams for a congregation are shattered or, worse yet, when we are demeaned by the very people we are trying to help, we become vulnerable to the myth of the greener grass. However, the grass on the other side of an ecclesiastical fence is usually not any better. Often it's shallow rooted and full of weeds. So when we're most tempted to jump ship, we must remember that there are no perfect churches.

I once heard Ray Stedman state, "In any body, a certain amount of body odor exists; it's true in the human body, and it's true in the local church." His observation is a reminder that pastors are called to serve a people who have both new and old natures. Since the old nature will not be eradicated until the day of Christ, unspiritual behavior should not surprise us. Depravity exists not only within a congregation but also, unfortunately, in pastors. Body odor is part and parcel of ministry, part of the call to service. Moving from Ohio to California will not eliminate the problem.

In all of my visits to the doctor's office, I've never heard a physician complain, "All I ever see is sick people! I'm tired of sick people. I'd rather deal with people who are healthy." This scenario is absurd because curing sickness is the very reason doctors practice medicine. If people never got ill, physicians wouldn't be needed.

Similarly, sickness of the soul generates the need for ministers. The reality of human depravity, even in our churches, necessitates the teaching and caregiving of the clergy. Therefore, it's naive and foolish to be surprised or immobilized by sick behavior in a church. A change in ministry will not change human nature. Perfect congregations do not exist.

#3: Decisions Made in the Absence of Objective Data Are Potentially Disastrous

Successful business executives perform annual audits. Responsible pilots continually confirm their bearings. Likewise, smart pastors should regularly evaluate their personal ministry direction and effectiveness. Honest input regarding your present service is a prerequisite when considering any change.

A systematic pastoral review, though somewhat intimidating, is a helpful tool for measuring congregational fit. In reality, a pastoral evaluation is a two-way observation. The board's assessment of the pastor, in turn, provides a means for the minister to measure the church. The appraisal process reveals the congregation's values, priorities, and needs. Through it, we can see if their values and goals are the same as ours and weigh how well we are responding to their needs. A decision to stay or leave is more wisely made in light of data gathered through objective evaluation. Periodic assessments can confirm that we're on the right course or indicate that corrections are needed.

Although regular, systematic appraisals provide useful data, they are ill-advised during crises. As one pastor warned, "If you've never had evaluations, don't start them when a problem exists." Appraisals made during difficult times are frequently clouded by subjectivity and are negative in value. But regular assessments enable both pastor and lay leaders to measure more accurately the degree of "fit" with a congregation. Wise stewardship profits from periodic assessment. Getting the facts lets pastors know how well they are doing. Therefore, a decision about moving is unwise if it is made in the absence of that information.

#4: Selective Perception Limits Our Understanding of Reality

Psychologists tell us that people see things as they *think* they are or as they think they *want* them to be. This coloring of objectivity is known as *selective perception*. A baseball manager's arguing with an umpire illustrates this phenomenon, as do the different versions of *the truth* told to a marital counselor by a husband and wife. Although it's tough to admit, pastors, too, are vulnerable to the effects of distorted vision.

I once served on a church staff where four pastors played racquetball together three times a week. On one occasion, Dave served the ball and I called it short. His partner, Don, thought it was good, but Rick saw it my way. What do you do when four clerics, located in different places on the court, none of whom is trying to cheat, can't agree on whether a blue ball was north or south of a red line? Well, you play the point over again; ordination doesn't eliminate biased thinking.

Availing ourselves of the observations of others is a wise move when we are considering a change in ministry. As one district minister expressed it, "One thing about our blind spots is that we can't see them. Therefore, we have to trust someone else. We have to put our faith in an objective, trustworthy person who will help us see things as they are, so that we can see ourselves as we are. Without this kind of mirroring, we get in trouble." A decision based solely on our own assessment is potentially disastrous.

In the chapters that follow, a number of "congregational signals," "personal signals," and "pastor/people signals" describe red lights (warnings to stay) or green lights (permission to move). Most likely, you will first consider these indicators by yourself. But shortly thereafter you will want to ask family members for their input. Then, to add further objectivity to your analysis, work through the criteria with a couple of confidants who both know you and the church well.

Proverbs 15:22 reminds us, "Plans fail for lack of counsel, but with many advisors they succeed." The objective counsel of others can help us determine whether a decision to remain or move is best. Taking advantage of their input minimizes the distorting effect of selective perception.

#5: Evaluative Criteria Are Guidelines, Not Mandates

Exact formulas for determining the rightness of a move are impossible to establish. Fail-safe guidelines for transition are nonexistent, so beware of using simplistic measuring devices that promise guidance. In my files, for example, I have two short instruments that claim to offer such direction. Respondents simply have to answer yes or no to a series of nine questions to determine whether to *unpack your bags* or *send out your resume.*

Although such devices are appealing, they are overly simplistic. Critical variables, such as family contentment, are glaringly absent from the criteria. Furthermore, the same weight is assigned to each variable, when in reality the importance of a particular item varies from person to person.

For this reason, the transition criteria presented in this book are set on a continuum. The reader is allowed to make directional assessments without getting into an either/or, yes/no trap. The format also allows a pastor to assign varying weights to the items. By the time the thirty-five factors (signals) are considered, a directional pattern tends to emerge regarding fit with one's present church and a calling congregation. Nevertheless, even this comprehensive process is not inerrant, so your decision must be tempered by the fact that evaluative criteria are guidelines, not mandates.

Let me conclude with a question: Are you reading this book on a Monday? If so, perhaps you should put it down until later in the week. Or at least please reread this chapter with your spouse before proceeding. Perhaps for you a change in ministry may be just what the doctor ordered, especially if you can move positively toward an opportunity of great fit. On the other hand, maybe it's better for you to remain in your present position for now. As you proceed through the inquiry, please keep these warnings in mind; they can serve as a safeguard against making an ill-advised decision.

Know who is in control + Know when it is free will

2

SOVEREIGN DIRECTION
AND PERSONAL CHOICE

IN YOUR HANDS YOU HOLD A BOOK THAT offers guidance for wise decision making. In essence, it's a compendium of counsel woven together from the stories of hundreds of ministry colleagues. It provides signals, charts, and questions to help you assess your ministry service. But before you begin your study, you may be thinking, W*ait a minute. Where is God in this process? What is my part and what is His part in a transition, or a call to ministry, for that matter?* Let's begin with this query.

Recently, I reviewed a dozen books on the call to ministry. The authors, both classical and contemporary, agreed that all Christians are called to minister. Believers are to follow the example of Jesus, who "came not to be ministered unto, but to minister" (Mark 10:45 KJV). We have been commissioned to make disciples (Matt. 28:19–20) and therefore given "the ministry of reconciliation" (2 Cor. 5:18). God produces fruit in Christians' lives so that they may nurture others (Gal. 5:22–23). The Spirit also endows them with a complementary array of spiritual gifts so that they may serve one another (1 Cor. 12). In reality, all Christians are called into full-time Christian service.

The authors differed, however, on whether there exists *a special call* into career service or professional ministry. Some of the writers argued that no one ever chooses the pastorate; God always initiates this career call. Many of our colleagues agree with this assessment. As one expressed it, "I felt like there was nothing else I could do." Or in the words of another, "God wrapped His steely hand around my soul and claimed me for ministry."

However, other writers presented the case that God welcomes all who *choose* to enter a Christian service career. They concurred with the apostle that "if anyone sets his heart on being an overseer, he desires a noble task" (1 Tim. 3:1). Again, many of our colleagues agree with this understanding. For example, one pastor stated, "God wired me a builder, and I believe he has given me the freedom to build a great business if I so desire. But I have chosen to use that gift mix within the church." Another colleague expressed it thus: "As a collegian, I planned to be a high-school guidance counselor. However, during those years, I was heavily involved in the leadership of my church's youth ministry, and my heart pulled more and more toward Christian service. I felt, 'Why should I work all week in one job, when I really enjoy this area of discipleship better?' For that reason, I went to seminary and later accepted a youth pastorate upon graduation."

Why is it that scholars disagree on the nature of God's call, whether it's a call into ministry or involves a change in ministry direction? I believe the answer is that our humanity simply cannot comprehend divine paradox. We always push toward the either/or, when God frequently provides the both/and.

Paradoxes That Perplex

How can we reconcile the two apparently contradictory doctrines of sovereign direction and free will as they pertain to decision making? Perhaps if we look at several other Christian doctrines we can discover implications for our study.

Did you ever wonder how a clever heresy becomes established? The best way is to begin with a sound teaching, then push it so far to an extreme that it denies a companion doctrine. While the human mind seeks simplicity and closure, faith and biblical integrity require acceptance of theological paradoxes that sometimes perplex.

The Triune Nature of God

The doctrine of the Trinity taxes the understanding of most people. It seems more logical to believe in only one God, or even to accept polytheism, than to affirm that one God exists simultaneously in three persons. Nevertheless, this view alone is supported by Scripture.

Both the Old and the New Testaments teach that God is one and that there is no other but Him (e.g., Deut. 6:4; Mark 12:29, 32). God alone is eternal, omniscient, holy, just, good, merciful, and so on. Only God is creator and sustainer of the universe. But as we examine the biblical evidence, we discover that those divine qualities and acts are attributed to the Father (Matt. 6:8; John 17:11; Rom. 16:26–27; 1 Cor. 8:6); to the Son, Jesus Christ (John 16:30; Acts 3:14; Col. 1:15–16; Heb. 1:8, 12); and to the Holy Spirit (Job 33:4; John 14:26; 1 Cor. 2:10; Heb. 9:14).

Although it might be easier for finite minds to embrace the monotheism of Islam or the polytheism of Mormonism, true biblicists must embrace a Trinitarian theology. The scriptural evidence affirms the triune nature of God.

The Deity-Humanity of Christ

The Bible doesn't teach that Jesus is part human and part divine; it asserts that He is fully man and fully God. This is another paradox that perplexes. Jesus' humanity was observable during His earthly sojourn: He hungered, thirsted, was tired, wept, and died. "Since the children have flesh and blood, he too shared in their humanity" (Heb. 2:14). Nevertheless, His divine nature was not lost in the incarnation. Followers and critics alike recognized His godliness and power: "'We are not stoning you for any of these [miracles],' replied the Jews, 'but for blasphemy, because you, a mere man, claim to be God'" (John 10:33). Although it is difficult to understand how Jesus can be simultaneously fully God and fully man, the Bible affirms His dual nature.

The Divine-Human Authorship of Scripture

Both internal and external evidence point to divine authorship of the Bible: "All Scripture is God-breathed and is useful for teaching, rebuking, correcting and training in righteousness" (2 Tim. 3:16). Yet the Bible clearly represents—and textual criticism reveals—a diversity of human authorship. Moses, Solomon, Ezekiel, Luke, Paul, and Peter are just a few of the writers who recorded God's revelations and acts. Evidently, God used the vocabulary, grammar, and style of individuals to pen His truth. Yet He superintended the human process to preserve His divine message (see 2 Peter 1:20–21).

When we ask, "How did God do this?" we conclude that in our finiteness we can never fully comprehend the infinite Sovereign. Nevertheless, we affirm the paradox of the divine-human authorship of Scripture.

The Biblical View of Salvation

How is a person saved? Does God elect certain people to eternal life, or do they appropriate forgiveness through repentance and faith? Whereas some Christians emphasize the verses supporting sovereign choice (explaining away human accountability), others point to the Scriptures on free will (softening predestination with foreknowledge, for example). Yet, a comprehensive look at the biblical evidence leads to the conclusion that salvation involves the actions of both God and humanity. We must balance Ephesians 1:4 ("For he chose us in him before the creation of the world") and Romans 10:13 ("Everyone who calls on the name of the Lord will be saved"). God's sovereign election does not negate an individual's responsibility to receive Christ.

Eternal Security and Perseverance

Who is responsible to maintain a person's salvation? This, too, is a perplexing paradox. Verses such as Hebrews 10:26–27 teach human responsibility: "If we deliberately keep on sinning after we have received the knowledge of the truth, no sacrifice for sins is left, but only a fearful expectation of judgment and of raging fire that will consume the enemies of God." But verses such as Philippians 1:6 emphasize God's responsibility in this area: "Being confident of this, that he who began a good work in you will carry it on to completion until the day of Christ Jesus." Does the Bible affirm eternal security? Most definitely! Does it teach personal perseverance? Yes!

Divine/Satanic Control of the World

Who is in control? Here is still another doctrine held in tension. For example, "The LORD does whatever pleases him, in the heavens and on the earth, in the seas and all their depths" (Ps. 135:6) does not harmonize with, "We know that we are children of God, and that the whole world is under control of the evil one" (1 John 5:19). These verses, like others, recognize two sources of power. We may argue that Satan's dominion is within God's control, but the bottom line is that both have authority in this world. When adverse circumstances come our way, are they from God or from Satan? The evidence suggests that it could be either—or both.

In light of these major doctrinal paradoxes, it should not surprise us that daily Christian living is also a joint divine/human venture. Consider the following verses from Paul's letters:

> I have been crucified with Christ and I no longer live, but Christ lives in me. The life I live in the body, I live by faith in the Son of God, who loved me and gave himself for me. (Galatians 2:20)

> Continue to work out your salvation with fear and trembling, for it is God who works in you to will and to act according to his good purpose. (Philippians 2:12a–13)

> To this end I labor, struggling with all his [Christ's] energy, which so powerfully works in me. (Colossians 1:29)

Is the Christian responsible to live a life honoring to God? Yes, of course. But does God live this life, *His* life, through the believer? Again, a resounding yes! Therefore, it should not surprise us that the call to career service is also both God's direction and our personal choice.

An Analogy from Flight

The harmonizing of our responsibility for decision making with God's sovereign guidance is perhaps best understood by way of analogy.

The Christian life may be likened to air travel. Each of us sits in the cockpit of our own plane, with our ultimate destination that of Christlikeness and the eternal kingdom. Sometimes the journey is smooth; sometimes we encounter turbulence. Nevertheless, in spite of a variety of aeronautical conditions, we are responsible for how well we navigate through our Christian life and handle the plane's instruments.

Some people teach that God wants us to let go of the stick and let him take full control of our lives. They point to Ephesians 5:18: "Be filled with the Spirit," and interpret it, *Be controlled by the Spirit*. Following this understanding, for example, I was taught to exhale sin (confession) and inhale the Holy Spirit (the filling) and that it was through prayer that the Spirit would control me.

But not too long after going through such a procedure, I would sin again. Since God didn't cause me to sin, my only conclusion was that I must have retaken control of my life. So I confessed my sin and asked God to control me again. But then I sinned again—and so the story goes repeatedly.

Unfortunately, taking my hands off the stick and letting God fly the plane alone didn't work. Furthermore, this understanding of the Spirit-filled life is not the best interpretation about Scripture. Jesus' parable of the talents and Paul's instruction on the judgment seat of Christ both teach that I will be judged not on the degree to which I took my hands off the controls but on how well I handled the stick.

God expects me to fly my Christian life, and He holds me accountable to do so. God doesn't want to be the pilot of my life, nor does He expect to sit in the co-pilot's seat with both of us fighting over the controls. Rather, the Lord operates two ways in my life.

First, He places *within* my cockpit a Chief Navigator. Every Christian is indwelt by the Holy Spirit, the same Spirit who inscripturated the truth of the Bible and illumines our minds to its truth. The Spirit opens the charts and says, "John, if you want to get to your destination and have a safe flight, follow these charts." Although He doesn't force me to travel in a particular direction, He does guide me. I can choose to ignore the Navigator's charts and leading and fly by the seat of my pants, but if I do so, I'll pay the price. Rather than taking over the controls of my life, He asks me to fly according to His guidance. I am 100 percent responsible for making wise decisions throughout the flight.

Second, beyond the influence of the Holy Spirit within the cockpit, God is sovereignly at work *outside* of my aircraft. Recently, when I was flying back to the Twin Cities, the pilot announced, "We'll be twenty minutes late arriving into Minneapolis; we're bucking a stiff head wind." On another trip, my plane arrived early because of a tail wind. And on one memorable occasion, the craft lost altitude quickly, causing the flight attendant to dump a pot of coffee on the passenger next to me. Air turbulence quickly reminds pilots that the conditions surrounding them critically affect their journey.

Similarly, God is constantly at work in my life through sovereign circumstances. Sometimes, He gives me a tail wind, and everything seems to go smoothly. At other times, He allows turbulence or a challenging head wind. Nevertheless, this reality doesn't negate my responsibility to fly to my best ability and according to the charts of the Navigator.

Who, then, is responsible for our decision making? To what degree can pastors use objective criteria to make vocational choices, and to what degree is God behind those choices? Clearly, God holds pastors accountable for making responsible ministry decisions, yet He constantly reminds us that he is also at work, bringing "to completion" that which He has begun (Phil. 1:6).

When considering a call to professional ministry or a career transition, read carefully the external environment, knowing that God is the Lord of circumstances. While doing so, take comfort in knowing that the Holy Spirit is interceding on your behalf and that He is the author of peace. Because He has also designed and given you counselors to share advice, you can fly with confidence, taking control of the stick, trusting the Navigator's charts, and paying attention to the lights on the instrument panel.

The Big Four Convergence

Now we have come full circle back to the original question: How do you know that God is in this vocational call or transition before you? How do you know if this is a "both/and" situation or if you are just out there by yourself, doing some wishful thinking? If you listened to the stories of ministry colleagues, several common themes would appear. Four factors seem always present in the divine–human interaction of decision making: compulsion, character, competencies, and confirmation.

Compulsion

Colleagues who survive in professional ministry frequently attribute their effectiveness to their sense of call. Those who lean toward the God side of the equation refer to this as a divine unction whereas those who lean toward the human side of the equation refer to it as a deep desire or passion. Some pastors feel that they just can't do anything else. Others believe that they could but just don't want to. All of them are sold out 100 percent to kingdom building. This is what turns them on; this is what they want to do as long as they have breath.

Character

No doubt you have heard the expression, "The Christian life is more caught than taught." Jesus Himself first had His disciples be *with* Him before He sent them out to preach (Mark 3:14). Lives are not transformed by merely hearing the verbiage of religious professionals. That did not happen in Christ's day, and it won't happen today. People are changed when they see how it's done in the lives of their leaders.

Just because a person desires to work in professional ministry (compulsion) doesn't mean that the individual is automatically qualified to serve. Although no one is perfect, Paul does use the umbrella qualification "above reproach" to affirm that godly character is important in ministry (1 Tim. 3:2). Pastors are expected to have a great relationship with their spouses and children. Likewise, they should have a healthy relationship with people both inside and outside of the church. Their motivation must never be money or status. Their deportment should be respectable, hospitable, and gentle. Leaders who best emulate these lifestyle qualities are most fit for service. Those who fail the character check, regardless of their desire, should not expect a remunerated ministry position. Whereas inner compulsion drives us toward service, godly character makes us fit for that service.

Competencies

Occasionally, I meet seminarians who view a Master of Divinity degree as a union card. They figure that someone owes them a church upon graduation. However, Christian organizations don't hire people who simply feel called to ministry. They exchange valuable donor dollars for very focused missional tasks. Therefore, in addition to the compulsion to serve and a solid Christian character, each particular ministry position requires specific competencies.

Some specialized roles require greater care-giving gifts (e.g. pastoral counseling) whereas others demand greater administrative abilities (e.g. children's ministry). Churches are also looking for individuals who are disciplined, loyal, self-starters, and team players who have vision and can handle criticism.

Occasionally, a referral will come to me with a qualifier: "I believe this person can be a great pastor if someone will take him under their wing for a couple of years." Unfortunately, although churches are willing to train interns, they only hire staff who already have the competencies to hit the ground running.

To have a passion for the Lord's work is wonderful. To have a love for Christ and a godly life is honorable. But, in addition, only those who have solid ministry competencies are marketable.

Confirmation

Every year, I meet individuals who believe that God wants them to work in a church but can't land a position. The obvious confirmation of one's ministerial call and ability is the offer of a job position.

Very often the confirmation process begins early in one's Christian life. As people serve, they find joy in using their gifts. Over time, others begin to notice their abilities and commend them on the work they are doing. It is not uncommon for an individual to hear: "Fred, have you thought about going into ministry?" Or, "Jill, you should think about going to seminary—I believe God could really use you in the church."

Affirmation from friends and mentors will confirm a call to ministry.

Summary

So how do we know if God is calling us to service or a ministry transition? Succinctly stated, when your internal desire encounters an external opportunity, you are probably on the right track. And when the four signs of compulsion, character, competencies, and confirmation converge in your life, you know that fruitful ministry is ahead.

3

ASSESSING YOUR
PRESENT MINISTRY
Congregational Signals

SOMETIMES I THINK WE MAKE THE Christian life overly mystical. Sure, the Bible speaks of mystery, but it also illustrates simplicity. Although it affirms that "the Lord determines [a person's] steps" (Prov. 16:9), it also assumes a sound decision-making process. Jesus said, "Suppose one of you wants to build a tower. Will he not first sit down and estimate the cost to see if he has enough money to complete it? . . . Or suppose a king is about to go to war against another king. Will he not first sit down and consider whether he is able with his ten thousand men to oppose the one coming against him with twenty thousand?" (Luke 14:28, 31).

Just as rationality is part of the *Imago Dei,* making choices is as naturally human as breathing. People make decisions about what to wear, what type of car to drive, where to live, whom to marry, what to fix for dinner, where to shop, and with whom to spend leisure time. Among the weightiest decisions a pastor must make is whether to seek a new place of ministry.

Before you can answer the question, "Is this new church right for me?" you must answer another question: "Do I have a freedom to leave my current congregation?" Pastors who are considering a change in service will profit greatly by first observing several signals in their present ministry.

Colleagues across our country have identified twenty significant factors that help assess one's present status in a particular pastorate. These signs cluster into three groups: congregational signals, personal signals, and pastor/people signals. Strong red lights from these signals remind us of the benefit of remaining in our present work whereas brilliant green lights give us a freedom to move on. Weak or neutral yellow signals tell us to be cautious.

Congregational signals in one's present ministry include the regulatory lights of spiritual appetite, congregational stability, trained laity, healthy attendance, and generosity.

Spiritual Appetite

Whether you have thirty-five years of ministry ahead of you or only five years until retirement, life is too short to pour your energies into a work where people just play church. Jesus said that only those who truly hunger and thirst for righteousness will find satisfaction (Matt. 5:6). So a bottom line question worth determining is: How spiritually hungry are my people? Are they more indifferent? Are they actively seeking Christian maturity?

If after a reasonable tenure of service your congregation still seems apathetic to spiritual growth, you might well consider a reinvestment of service where your efforts can have greater impact. On the other hand, if you find people eager to mature in Christ, then remaining to feed their responsiveness is an appropriate choice.

Pastors should not bail out of a situation simply because a few people do unspiritual things. After all, our calling is to help the entire flock mature. Nor should we feel discouraged if some folks seem complacent. The church as a whole should be your reference point. Since most ministries experience high and low moments, the key question is, "What's the overall temperature of my people? What is the general spiritual climate in the congregation?" Spiritual indicators include the following:

- Enthusiasm in worship
- Participation in Bible studies

- Depth of volunteerism
- Attentiveness to preaching
- Involvement in cell groups
- Assimilation of newcomers
- Caring for one another's needs
- Members sharing their faith
- Personal ministries beyond the congregation

Obviously, an honest reading of these factors requires contextual appraisal. If people are not *encouraged* to serve outside the church (in adoption agencies, prisons, shelters, etc.), they can't be criticized for weakness in this area. Preaching that lacks energy, structure, relevance, or adherence to the text will cause people to drift. A church that is trying to offer more programs than can be staffed might have a problem with expectations, not spirituality. Nevertheless, with a proper understanding of the context, the preceding criteria are useful in measuring the spiritual appetite of a congregation.

If you have worked both hard and wisely and the congregation shows signs of spiritual growth, consider this a red light that illumines the benefit of remaining. After all, it's easier to roll an object in the direction it's already moving than to try to initiate movement or reverse direction (perhaps your fate in a new congregation). But if your church seems stagnant or indifferent to spiritual things, this is a green light that signals the possibility of a productive move.

Congregational Stability

Most congregations view the pastor as their spiritual leader, their shepherd. Jesus affirmed, "The good shepherd lays down his life for the sheep. The hired hand is not the shepherd who owns the sheep. So when he sees the wolf coming, he abandons the sheep and runs away. Then the wolf attacks the flock and scatters it. The man runs away because he is a hired hand and cares nothing for the sheep" (John 10:11–13). Periodic reflection on our shepherding responsibilities is beneficial.

Although some members view the pastor as an employee and some ministers want to work only 9 to 5, most pastors consider themselves shepherds, not hirelings. We are not in this profession for the money but sincerely to touch lives for the kingdom. If we sense an instability or vulnerability in our congregation, we dare not run away like a hired hand. Our responsibility is to stay and protect the flock.

Red lights in this area are easily recognized. For example, one colleague suggested, "A pastor should not leave during a building program. He should remain for at least two years afterward." Whether an expansion fulfills a minister's dream or drains most of his or her energy, a congregation will feel betrayed if the pastor takes off too quickly. This is especially true if the church assumed a significant indebtedness over the expansion.

A second sign of congregational vulnerability is revealed by asking, "Are there problems I can help resolve?" Or, as one pastor expressed it, "If you are considering leaving because of problems, you need to try to determine the nature of the problem. If the problem is perennial in the church, it's probably better to stay and work it through rather than make the new pastor face it. If the problem is in relationship with you, it's probably better to leave."

Staff instability is another warning sign to consider. One senior pastor received an inquiry from an attractive church during the time his current congregation was experiencing serious problems with its youth pastor. Regretfully, he declined the opportunity because, as he expressed it, "I couldn't leave the congregation with this mess. We needed to handle the termination graciously, deal with the flak that followed, and then hire a new person who could reestablish the youth ministry."

Credibility is lost and trust is eroded when a pastor leaves after a sabbatical or moves shortly after completing a degree program that the church helped to finance. The congregation feels taken advantage of, and rightly so—and the next pastor will inherit distrust.

Churches are also vulnerable during and immediately after the adoption of a new constitution, the planting of a daughter church, a relocation, or a major change in programming (such as the redesign of worship or scheduling changes).

If you sense that your congregation is vulnerable for any of the preceding reasons, then this red light tells you that it's best to remain for the time being. If the congregation seems balanced and stable, this signal indicates freedom to move.

Trained Laity

The adequacy of trained lay leadership in a church is a third regulating signal. Paul's charge to Timothy is every pastor's admonition: "And the things you have heard me say in the presence of many witnesses entrust to reliable men who will also be qualified to teach others" (2 Tim. 2:2). The senior pastor who faces shortages of elders, deacons, or other leaders is probably seeing a red light regarding a move. The youth pastor who serves in the absence of sponsors, interns, or volunteer workers is in a similar situation. And the children's minister with vacancies in key program positions probably has work remaining in the present congregation. Inadequate leadership among the laity makes a church vulnerable during transition, especially if the church has a small staff.

A major part of the pastor's job is "to prepare God's people for works of service" (Eph. 4:12). Unfortunately, many pastors find themselves so busy doing the ministry that they lack sufficient time to train others. The problem is exacerbated when a church tries to offer an unrealistic amount of programming. One colleague reminds us, "Our churches can't afford to pay ministers to do the entire ministry. Congregations just don't have the finances to pay people to do all the things necessary to meet expressed needs."

Furthermore, since spiritual growth is a by-product of service, we dare not let only a few people reap the blessings of ministry to others. Christians grow and the church is strengthened when the children's pastor develops lay ministers to meet the needs of children and families; the associate pastor multiplies adult leaders for Bible classes and home cell groups; and the senior pastor trains lay pastors to care, counsel, visit, and even preach. Lay leadership keeps the body healthy and growing.

"Timing is everything," reflected one pastor, "and the timing of a move is related to the strength of our key leadership." This colleague shared how he periodically received inquiries from other congrega-tions, but that it wasn't until his church had a strong enough leader-ship base that he sensed a freedom even to consider a move. "When I came to the church, we couldn't find enough people to fill our va-cancies. But by the sixth year we had multiple candidates for most positions, with those serving exuding a confidence of ownership."

While the pastor is not the only one responsible for leadership de-velopment, equipping the saints for service is the heart of his or her task. A minister who cannot motivate others to lead, who cannot ac-complish ministry through others, should not transfer that inability to another congregation. It is far better to learn how to become more effective in one's present congregation or to transition completely out of professional service if that skill cannot be mastered.

In assessing a present ministry, a pastor should ask, "Will my de-parture significantly impair the oversight of this congregation?" The light of transition shines red in the absence of effective lay leadership. On the other hand, the existence of competent and confident laity indicates a freedom to seek a new ministry setting.

Healthy Attendance

One of the challenges in leaving my Southwest congregation to pastor on the east coast was to see if it was possible to grow a church in a fairly static, traditional community. Christ said, "I will build my church" (Matt. 16:18), and repeatedly in the book of Acts we see His servants adding to this body (2:47, 5:14, 6:7, 11:21; 16:5). In addition, He commands our participation—we are to "go and make disciples" (Matt. 28:19), regardless of the neighborhood. Thus, although nu-merical growth is not the only measure of church health, it is cer-tainly one indicator of ministry effectiveness. Although only a limited number of churches will ever grow to *mega* size, even the smallest of congregations can draw new people into its fellowship.

Community demographics affect, but do not determine, the size of a congregation. Some churches are alive and well; others are dying. Some churches have a vibrancy that makes them attractive to visitors; others are bland, unable to draw newcomers. Some churches are growing, even in shrinking neighborhoods; others are in decline in expanding communities.

A pastor in a growing situation might feel comfortable leaving the church when it's in such good shape. And if other signals confirm transition, a change may indeed be timely. But more often vibrancy and growth are a solid signal to remain. Since dynamic congregations are few and far between, a flourishing ministry is worth capitalizing on. Be cautious when you are considering departure from a blossoming work.

However, when your best efforts fail to enliven a church, perhaps it's time to concentrate your energies on a new challenge. As one colleague expressed it, "When a ministry stalls, basic statistics have leveled off or are in decline, and you haven't got a clue to why, it's probably time to move." Another pastor suggested that it's probably time "when the church has plateaued in growth and development, and you can't move them off the plateau." Another said, "The light is green when you have a sense that you've done all for the congregation you can do." Still another observed, "Pastors need to ask themselves, 'Is the church ready for a new chapter through which I can effectively lead them?' If the answer is no, a change may be the best thing for all concerned."

In summary, congregational vitality is an important measuring device for a pastor who is contemplating transition. If your flock is experiencing vibrancy and growth in response to your leadership, you probably should stay. Thousands of pastors would love such an opportunity! On the other hand, if stagnation or decline has set in and you lack the ability or desire to take the church any further, you probably are seeing a green light and are free to move elsewhere.

Generosity

Pastors who identify attendance as a "congregation signal" frequently mention finances as a companion signal. Numbers and dollars are never the ultimate measure of ministry, but people do express their appreciation or dissatisfaction through their investments of time and money.

Disgruntled members do not need to fight a pastor with words—their quiet withdrawal of contributions alone exerts an enormous amount of leverage. One district executive minister observed, "A conflict begins to reach crisis proportions when the members not only absent themselves from public service but also deliberately withhold contributions to force the issue. Ironically, sometimes contributions are higher after the pastor leaves than they were before he left, even if there was a loss of membership." The closing of a checkbook is not as loud as the vocal critic, but it may be felt more strongly.

Effective ministry requires growing financial resources. Whether the money is used for staff, programs, or facilities, dollars fuel ministry. Although a surplus in the annual budget may be a sign of health, it may also mean that a congregation just set too safe a fiscal goal. On the other hand, a shortfall may simply indicate unrealistically high expectations.

Jesus said, "Where your treasure is, there your heart will be also" (Matt. 6:21). Bountiful giving is an affirmation of ministry direction. It shows the people's approval of how their hard-earned dollars are spent. Generosity, therefore, is a signal to remain, suggesting that further expenditures of energy will bear additional fruit.

But when realistically set and normally reached budgets shrink considerably, beware! The withholding of normal giving indicates either disapproval of church goals or the existence of unanswered needs. The pastor whose church is experiencing a chronic shortfall or decline in needed resources may be seeing a green light that signals the advisability of a move. In some cases, staying may help people work through their concerns, but if remaining continues to fuel the problem, it's time to go.

Summary

When I drive toward a metered intersection, I usually don't ask God if He wants me to stop or proceed. I simply respond to the signal. If the light's green, I go ahead; if it's red, I remain where I am. Before the foundation of the world, God knew what color that light would be there when I arrived at the intersection. He is free to order

His world any way He desires, but that does not change my responsibility. Responsible driving requires my attention and proper response to obvious road signs.

Resigning from a present ministry and accepting a call to another church is an irreversible, life-changing decision. Gut feelings, friendly advice, and even prayer are insufficient for making a confident choice. But thankfully, God has also given us His Word, His Spirit, a sound mind, and clear signs for guidance. The congregational signals of spiritual appetite, congregational stability, trained laity, healthy attendance, and generosity are several of those regulatory signals that are worth heeding.

The assessment guide on the following page can help you identify directional responses to the congregational signals discussed in this chapter. As you mark each item on the continuum, notice whether your answers cluster toward the red-light side or the green-light side. You might find that you place a number of marks near the middle of the scale. In that case, a yellow light of caution warns you not to make any hasty decisions. But after completing this inventory (and the following guides on personal signals and pastor/people signals), many of you will see directional patterns emerge. These signals can shed light on whether the benefits of continuing in your present service outweigh the advantages of pursuing a change.

Assessing Your Present Ministry:
Congregational Signals

1. Congregational Hunger   _|_|_|_|_|_|_|_   Congregational Apathy

2. Congregational Vulnerability   _|_|_|_|_|_|_|_   Congregational Stability

3. Inadequate Lay Leadership   _|_|_|_|_|_|_|_   Abundant Trained Leadership

4. Vibrancy and Growth   _|_|_|_|_|_|_|_   Stagnation and Decline

5. Generous Giving   _|_|_|_|_|_|_|_   Shortage of Finances

4

ASSESSING YOUR
PRESENT MINISTRY
Personal Signals

RESPONSIBLE DRIVERS EXERCISE caution when arriving at an intersection. This same type of care should govern the actions of pastors when they are approaching a ministerial crossroad. Along with the congregational signals just examined, several personal signals offer equally valuable guidance. Safety surrounds the cleric who pays attention to the signals of personality, giftedness, job satisfaction, job challenge, future possibilities, opportunity for impact, family well-being, and adequacy of compensation. Again, any of these eight signals can flash red, advising you to slow down or stop, or shine green, encouraging you to proceed (with caution, of course).

Personality

A few months after I assumed a new pastorate, a man in my church commented, "Pastor, I heard a powerful sermon on the radio yesterday, and you know, the speaker didn't use humor even once." Now, I'm a pretty smart boy, and I realized that Pete wasn't just giving a sermon report. He believed a pastor ought to enter the pulpit with fear and trembling, and that obviously excluded the use of humor.

In general, I agree with Pete regarding the importance of pastoral dignity and decorum. But I also believe that humor is a valuable tool. Appropriate humor can lighten the soul, illustrate a principle, and diffuse the tension surrounding a heavy subject. Humor is important to me philosophically, but it's also part of my nature. Both heredity (parental funny genes) and environment (growing up on *The Three Stooges*) have contributed to who I am. Because it is impossible for me not to see the humorous side of just about any situation, curtailing my use of humor simply to please Pete would never work.

This example highlights only one character quality, yet each of us has dozens of such traits. Some people are outgoing; others are more private. Some people are thinkers; others are feelers. Some people like structure; others like flexibility. Some people explode with bursts of energy; others are steady Freddies. One person is an idealist; another is a pragmatist. One pastor prefers a daily hands-on approach; another wants notification and personal involvement only when problems arise.

Like Jeremiah, we acknowledge that God knew us before we were formed in the womb and set us apart before we were born (Jer. 1:5). Each of us is unique, having particular personality strengths and limitations. It follows that a minister serving in harmony with his or her own personality serves with authenticity, which, in turn, deepens trust within parishioners. Usually, the longer we serve a church, the more likely the congregation will understand, accept, and even reflect our personality. If we are free to be ourselves, we are in a strong position to influence lives for the kingdom. When sensing this type of acceptance of our God-given wiring, it's wise to stay put for additional fruitful service.

The personality fit criterion does not mean that everyone in the church has to like you. Nor can it justify a "that's-just-the-way-I-am" attitude. But if you feel overwhelmingly, *I just can't be me,* a change is probably worth exploring. As one colleague expressed it, "When factors or circumstances beyond your control put a cap on who you are, then maybe it's time to move."

Giftedness

Closely related to the signal of personality is the personal signal of giftedness. Since "we have different gifts, according to the grace given us" (Rom. 12:6), it's important to ask, "To what degree do my spiritual gifts and other abilities match the current needs of this church?"

Congregations, like people, move through life passages. Similarly, at each stage leadership needs to change. During the birth of a church, for example, an evangelist/planter is usually called. Down the road, a builder/developer may better advance the work. During yet another stage, a gifted administrator may be needed to update its organizational structure and operations. Later, a dynamic visionary can revitalize a plateaued work.

Most of us know successful colleagues who at one time or another seemed to hit a wall in their ministry. One pastor expressed it thus: "I felt I was starting to lose my voice as a catalystic leader. People were affirming my vision but not joining in to do the work." After prayer and careful evaluation, this man concluded, "Someone else would probably do a better job than I in taking the church through a new chapter."

To some degree, all of us must stretch beyond our comfort zones. Occasions arise when the gifted administrator must counsel or a skillful caregiver is expected to lead in decision making. Nevertheless, your spiritual enablements and skill developments can produce greater fruit in one type of congregation than in another. Just as most shepherds are not comfortable with ranching responsibilities, most ranchers are not as effective one-on-one with the sheep. Therefore, an assessment of your giftedness in relation to your present congregation is essential when considering a transition.

Three questions can guide your study of giftedness fit. First, *what are my two primary spiritual gifts, and to what degree am I now using them?* Books and inventories are available to enhance your understanding of where you shine, but the bottom line here is whether you are serving according to your strengths.

Second, *how often do I use natural endowments and skills in my present work?* Some people are good with numbers, so they understand charts and budgets; others are better with their hands. Some people move with ease among unbelievers; others enjoy political maneuvering. Some people are good managers of conflict; others are detail oriented.

God uses both natural endowments and personal experiences to shape an individual's unique talents. These abilities are also valid criteria for assessing giftedness match.

Third, *how does my leadership style match congregational expectations?* Does the church want a C.E.O. or a colleague? Do the members prefer a systems developer or an influencer? A number of instruments (such as the Personal Profile System—DiSC[1]) can help you understand your personal style. Combined with this self-awareness, the simple observation of people's reactions to you can reveal much about the acceptability of your style.

Pastoral ministry involves a diversity of tasks. Although we are called to preach, teach, counsel, visit, manage, and be caregivers, admittedly we are not equally effective in all of those areas. Therefore, the degree of giftedness fit is an essential signal for transition guidance. If harmony exists between our personal giftedness and congregational expectations, this red light signals the benefits of remaining. Our most fruitful ministry may be just ahead in our own back yard. But if the church seems to require gifts and abilities that are not our forte, pursuing a new direction is probably a good decision.

Job Satisfaction

Just as road signs are strategically located to guide and protect us on our journeys, direction and safety information are available to pastors who heed the related signs of job satisfaction, job challenge, and future possibilities. All three factors yield a reading of our sense of accomplishment. Of the three signals, the one most easy to interpret is probably job satisfaction.

Enthusiasm as a ministry validator is not new. In the Gospels we observe that "the seventy-two [workers] returned with joy" (Luke 10:17) and that even amid persecution "the disciples were filled with joy" (Acts 13:52). The degree of our job satisfaction reveals how well our vocational needs and desires are being fulfilled. This moves us beyond the specifics of our tasks and queries how we feel about what we're doing. Periodically things go well, and time seems to fly; at other times they fall apart, and we feel unproductive and at a standstill. Finding joy in our work moves us toward people, but dissatisfaction leads us to withdrawal.

In spite of hardships, crises, and occasional misunderstandings, if you still have enthusiasm for your task, the red light of job satisfaction suggests that you should continue to serve in such a profitable environment. This was the conclusion of one pastor, who beamed, "Sometimes I just sit in my office and silently say, 'This is great! I love it and can't think of anything else I'd rather be doing. Thanks, God.'"

But if your experience is more like the pastor who admitted, "If I could feed my family any other way, I'd be gone tomorrow," then a move is critical. When ministry robs you of joy and it drains your vibrancy, then the green light of dissatisfaction releases you to pursue a change.

Getting an accurate reading on job satisfaction is complicated because all ministries have their difficult and discouraging moments. In fact, recent polls rank parish ministry among the most difficult professions. Nevertheless, while the ministry will always be taxing, the ratio of ups to downs or joys to discouragement provides insight. The degree to which enthusiasm or discouragement is your daily experience indicates how appropriate a move might be.

Job Challenge

Another important personal signal is an evaluation of the nature and size of your present assignment and whether you are able—and willing—to "make the most of every opportunity" (Col. 4:5). Although some things in your job description are probably more stimulating than others, consider the overall challenge of your job. Does it match your abilities and level of drive?

Some pastors have never seriously considered a move because they've sensed an ongoing fulfillment right in their present ministry. This was the feeling of one colleague who, in his twenty-third year at the church, related, "Though we temporarily plateaued a few times, I never got tired of the challenge of leading the congregation through a new chapter."

The experience of other pastors, however, is quite different. Feeling either overwhelmed or bored, many pastors have chosen to get a fresh start. One pastor expressed his frustration thus: "Every day was like drinking from a fire hose; I was in way over my head." Stretched beyond capacity, he eventually transitioned to a new church. Such situations led one denominational leader to conclude, "When the church grows past the ability, skills, training, and adaptability of its pastor, and the minister begins to feel inadequate, the 'Peter Principle' suggests it's time for a change."

On the other hand, most of our associates who have moved in response to this signal made their transition because they felt underutilized. As one friend explained, "The congregation was so affirming, it would have been easy for me to coast. But for my own growth I felt I needed a new situation where I'd have to be my very best." This pastor's decision paralleled the advice of two other colleagues. The first pastor observed, "When you realize you are no longer growing in a situation, or you've taken the church as far as you can, it's time to move." The second pastor suggested, "When a minister grows beyond the challenge of his church, he should start planning to move."

Pastors receiving an inquiry should ask themselves which church presents the greater challenge. Some ministers are continually challenged where they are whereas others find a tremendous challenge in moving to a new opportunity. Clergy who find their work stimulating sense an important reason for remaining with their congregation. Those who are faced with a job that's either mundane or overpowering, however, often profit from a move.

Future Possibilities

"Where there is no vision, the people perish" (Prov. 29:18 KJV), and without a dream, a pastor merely *parishes*. Neither minister nor congregation should tolerate simply "doing church." We're reminded, "Be very careful, then, how you live—not as unwise, but as wise, making the most of every opportunity" (Eph. 5:15–16). Although the signal of future possibilities is positioned beyond the signals of job satisfaction and job challenge, it requires a present assessment of opportunities that may lie ahead.

The pastor who envisions new programs, targeting new audiences, and strategizing daughter churches has good reason to remain with his or her present congregation. As one minister stated bluntly, "When God gives you a dream and it's not yet finished, you'd better stay." This red light is especially brilliant for the pastor who has sufficient credibility to pull off the dream.

But as another colleague suggests, "When the fire is gone and the creative juices are zapped, it's probably time to begin looking." Pastors without dreams lose their present effectiveness and their hope for the church's future. One friend admitted, "My feelings at that point included a difficulty in futurizing. I found it impossible to think in terms of any kind of vision." Another pastor confessed, "I got to the point in my relationship with the church that when I went calling on a healthy family that had visited us, I urged them to go to one of the churches nearby." When bright dreams are replaced by darkness, a move may preserve the health of both the cleric and congregation.

Finding joy in our work is important. Seeing possibilities ahead is also motivational. Where ideas and dreams are intact, wisdom suggests stopping and enjoying such possibilities. But if internal drive, motivation, and vision to take the church through another chapter is lost, as one minister put it, it's probably time to move elsewhere.

Opportunity for Impact

Most of us would not invest in a savings account yielding 3 percent interest if we could find one offering a 10 percent return. Neither is it prudent to spend fifty to sixty hours a week in a low-yield ministry if a higher return on our investment is possible. It makes sense to serve the Lord wherever we can make the greatest contribution. For the apostle Paul, this occasionally meant remaining in one place: "But I will stay on at Ephesus until Pentecost, because a great door for effective work has opened to me" (1 Cor. 16:8–9). At other times, a greater opportunity for discipleship meant a move. As one pastor summarized, "The point is that we just don't want to do what is comfortable; we want to change lives."

Now, opportunity for impact doesn't necessarily imply serving a larger church. For example, one senior pastor of a multiple-staff church accepted a solo, rural pastorate to carry on a broader ministry. Over the years, he had become an accomplished author, touching thousands of lives through the written word. Moving to a church with fewer programs and pressures allowed him to continue both shepherding and writing.

Assessing your opportunity for impact means that you stay or move according to whichever situation maximizes your outreach. I know one associate pastor who receives more than a dozen letters of inquiry a year, but now, in his sixth year at the church, he still states, "I can't see myself doing anything more significant than I'm doing right here." But for another associate minister, this signal meant moving to a senior pastorate where he could preach more regularly and give leadership to an entire flock. Another colleague left a senior pastorate to work in a staff position where he could disciple a burgeoning ministry for adults. Still another pastor moved to a seminary classroom where a passion for the local church could be ignited among young theologians.

Change for change's sake is usually unwise. A high-impact ministry in your present church suggests that you remain in this significant sphere of influence. But if greater outreach is possible elsewhere, you should not fear proceeding through this green light. To quote one of our colleagues, "You need to have a fair estimate of your abilities and honorable motives, but if you want to do more for God than you are presently doing, go for it."

Family Well-being

This signal is fairly easy to read. Whereas size of impact or giftedness may require deliberation, family contentment, or the lack thereof, is usually obvious.

At one end of the well-being continuum, family members are blossoming and free to be themselves. They feel loved and esteemed as the first family of the congregation. Perhaps the children receive special favors or the family is encouraged to vacation at a parishioner's cabin. More significantly, acceptance is felt through the regular smiles and verbal affirmations of the congregation.

At the other end of this spectrum, a pastor's family feels stifled and distressed. Unrealistic expectations placed on the pastor, the pastor's spouse, or their children erode ministry joy. One clergy spouse, feeling the sting of rejection, commented, "Living in a fish bowl is bad enough. But if the keepers of the aquarium don't even like the kind of fish that are in the bowl, why even bother swimming?" A suffering, dysfunctional family depletes joy and effectiveness in the home and at work. In such situations, a transition to another church can help the family recuperate and grow.

Care and management of our families is essential to ministry effectiveness (1 Tim. 3:5). And being in a caring congregation is essential to family well-being. So if you find yourselves identifying with the pastor who said, "I love how they make my kids feel special," remaining at your present church is probably a wise choice. But if your experience is more like the colleague who conceded, "We couldn't stay any longer—my wife was increasingly unhappy, close to a nervous breakdown—and I wasn't too far behind her," a green light is signaling that a move is probably just down the road.

Adequacy of Compensation

Pastors cannot expect to get rich through church service, but neither should they become impoverished. When serious financial pressures persist, we must first determine whether they are caused by inadequate compensation from the congregation or poor financial management on our part. If our money shortage is due to financial ineptness or poor discipline, a move will not resolve the problem. But a change may be appropriate when a shortfall of funds persists in spite of careful fiscal management.

A fair wage is not one that supports all of our financial wants and perceived needs. For example, I know pastors who have requested salary adjustments because they purchased a new car, had another baby, or enrolled a child in a Christian school. Their requests may have been based on financial need, but the expectation that the church should meet their every need was unrealistic. If their counterparts employed in the corporate world had approached their employees with similar requests (e.g., asking for a $4,000 salary increase to pay tuition at a Christian school), they would have been ridiculed. Adequacy of compensation is a valid signal when sound financial management is present and contextual variables are considered.

Congregations use many formulas to determine appropriate compensation for their pastoral staff. Among the more common practices are the following:

- Using averages of comparably sized churches within the denomination
- Keying staff salaries to local administrative and teaching scales (some churches multiply this figure by twelve-tenths, thus accommodating the clergy's additional months of yearly service)
- Comparing salaries with other churches in similar socio-geographical situations
- Relating remuneration to typical salaries in the congregation
- Setting the senior pastor's salary at a level equivalent to that of a white-collar executive in the congregation, with associate pastors receiving approximately 75 percent of that salary
- Adapting results from national surveys to the local context[2] (see figs. 1 and 2 at the end of this chapter)

Appropriate remuneration is the obligation of a church (1 Tim. 5:18), and providing financially for one's family is expected of the clergy (1 Tim. 3:4–5). The signal of adequacy of compensation asks you to assess the dollar exchange you receive for the time and effort you invest. A district supervisor tells pastors, "You have a biblical responsibility to face up to finances. If the church is not adequately meeting finances—given the fact that you are a wise manager of money—it may be time to move." But if the compensation package provided by a congregation is appropriate, or even generous, the pastor is seeing another red light and has reason to remain.

Summary

The overall question to be answered by heeding the eight personal signals examined in this chapter is "Can *I*, rather than some other pastor, serve in this church as a good steward?" Here the emphasis is on the *I*, the personal qualities and considerations that may or may not make it suitable for you to minister in one particular church rather than another.

The following chart will help you assess your degree of personal match with your present church. Again, as you did with the chart after chapter 3, note where your rankings cluster. Do you see more red lights than green lights? More green than red? Or, if your answers lie in the middle range of the continuum, do you see the yellow warning signal that a hasty decision may be dangerous?

Assessing Your Present Ministry:
Personal Signals

6. Authenticity
   Accepted
   _\|_\|_\|_\|_\|_\|_\|__
   Stifled Personality

7. Good Giftedness
   Match
   _\|_\|_\|_\|_\|_\|_\|__
   Poor Giftedness
   Match

8. Enthusiasm for
   the Task
   _\|_\|_\|_\|_\|_\|_\|__
   Restlessness or
   Withdrawal

9. Challenging
   Work
   _\|_\|_\|_\|_\|_\|_\|__
   Job Mundane or
   Overwhelming

10. More Dreams
    and Visions

    Silence or
    Nightmares

11. Good Opportunity
    for Impact
    _\|_\|_\|_\|_\|_\|_\|__
    Limited Opportunity
    for Impact

12. Family Happy
    and Growing

    Family Distressed
    and Stifled

13. Appropriate
    Compensation

    Insufficient
    Compensation

Figure 1

Total Compensation Comparisons of Senior Pastor by Church Setting

For Church Size: 251–500

	Urban	Suburban	Medium City	Small Town	Rural
Average attendance	394	374	369	359	361
Average church income	985,530	682,416	670,835	589,390	518,426
Average years employed	11	11	9	11	12
Average compensation*	96,725	79,992	70,645	75,239	72,000
Standard deviation	32,615	17,093	20,101	25,419	14,136
Median compensation	89,500	76,564	68,988	70,650	69,000

National average: $73,230 with a standard deviation of $30,128
Total respondents: 217

*Includes base salary, housing or parsonage allowance, retirement contribution, life and health insurance payments, and educational funds.[1]

1. James F. Cobble Jr. and Richard R. Hammar, *The 2004 Compensation Handbook for Church Staff* (Matthews, N.C.: Christian Ministry Resources, 2003), 45.

Figure 2

Total Compensation Comparisons of Youth Minister by Church Setting

For Church Size: Under 500

	Urban	Suburban	Medium City	Small Town	Rural
Average attendance	351	302	267	308	241
Average church income	939,846	590,482	474,350	524,103	397,551
Average years employed	3	3	3	4	3
*Average compensation**	44,907	43,118	36,216	42,767	37,480
Standard deviation	11,132	10,009	9,824	11,797	7,935
Median compensation	43,400	43,096	35,161	40,896	35,520

National average: $47,058 with a standard deviation of $14,492
Total respondents: 199

*Includes base salary, housing or parsonage allowance, retirement contribution, life and health insurance payments, and educational funds.[1]

---

1. James F. Cobble Jr. and Richard R. Hammar, *The 2004 Compensation Handbook for Church Staff* (Matthews, N.C.: Christian Ministry Resources, 2003), 45.

5

ASSESSING YOUR PRESENT MINISTRY
Pastor/People Signals

AT THIS POINT, IT MIGHT BE HELPFUL to review the meaning of the noun *signal*: "A signal is a sign or means of communication agreed upon or understood, and used to convey information . . . anything that incites to action or movement."[1]

This definition explains the task before us. In developing criteria for determining the appropriateness of a change in ministry, we have examined a number of factors to be considered at a point of transition. These signals convey information that moves us to action, even if that action is to apply the brakes. A pattern of red lights keeps us focused on our present ministry; a series of green lights propels us toward a new destination.

An examination of seven pastor/people signals will complete the assessment of one's present ministry. These interpersonal signals include compatibility of background, duration of tenure, strength of primary relationships, credibility level, degree of unity and support, pastoral evaluation, and advisors' counsel.

Compatibility of Background

As toddlers, my children enjoyed playing with puzzles. One toy of particular interest required the placing of various-shaped objects into their respective openings. The circular piece would fit into only the circular hole, the triangle slid through only the triangular opening, and the star fit only the star-shaped hole. Trying to find the compatible fit was difficult for the children until trial-and-error and maturing perception taught them the principle involved.

Trying to find a complementary pastor/congregation ministry match may be an even greater challenge. Discerning a good church fit is difficult not only because congregations differ greatly in their history and makeup but also because pastors' backgrounds vary even more.

Ministers come in many shapes. Their unique persons bear the mark of cultural stamping; each is shaped by his or her roots. For example, one of my minister friends was reared in a home where servants catered the family's meals. Another grew up eating chicken with his fingers, unsure of which fork to use at a formal dinner. Some ministers drove a tractor on the family farm while others played on city playgrounds. Some pastors experienced a friendly, affirming environment; others had a more aloof, impersonal upbringing. Some of our colleagues regularly attend the symphony and golf at a country club; others prefer pizza with the gang after a softball game. The sociocultural background of pastors varies greatly.

Congregations likewise differ one from another. For example, some churches schedule a clean-up day where volunteers restripe the parking lot, trim shrubbery, and clean windows; others contract out those services, never even thinking of asking members to take on such duties. In some churches, ownership of decision making is held at the grassroots level; in other congregations, a few representatives hold such powers. Churches vary in their sociocultural identities and traditions and in the primary expectations they develop. Trying to match pastoral background with congregational background is a challenge for even the best of search committees.

Ignoring background compatibility can be costly. For example, some of our colleagues have worn jeans and boots into a business-suited community, moved from a farming town to suburbia, left a one thousand-member California church to lead a two hundred-member Midwest congregation, migrated from a laid-back Southern pastorate to New England formality, and moved from a city ministry in Chicago to a rural work in Arkansas. Although some pastors can survive such culture shock, many will struggle with background fit.

Flexibility is a valuable characteristic for pastors. Becoming all things to all people for the gospel's sake is important in discipleship (1 Cor. 9:19–23). However, we can flex only so much. Each of us carries certain economic, geographic and social imprints that affect receptivity of our ministry. The more closely these backgrounds match the congregation we serve, the more likely the chance for deeper understanding and cooperation within the church. One pastor expressed it thus: "Who you are as the pastor has a great deal to do with the people you'll be able effectively to reach and touch. Some of you need to ask yourselves, 'Am I in the right place?'"[2]

A trapezoidal pastor ministering in a trapezoidal church serves with congruity; an oval pastor inside a rectangular church struggles. Good compatibility of background casts a red light on transition whereas poor sociocultural fit may be a reason to move.

Duration of Tenure

Although pastors can influence a church during even a brief ministry, most of our colleagues believe that their best accomplishments happened after their fourth year of service. A number of them identified years six to eight as the most rewarding. Church analysts laud extended pastorates, attributing plateau and decline to shorter tenures. Their conviction is that a pastor should stay in one place long enough to reach maximum impact but then should consider leaving shortly after the most effective years are realized.

Situations do occasionally arise when a pastor finds it necessary to make a change, even after a brief term of service. For example, one pastor moved because "a family problem required us to leave the geographical area." Another pastor admitted, "My situation was so bad I just had to leave, so I jumped at the first offer that came." Another related, "It took me only three months to realize the situation was not resolvable. At least twelve families had left the church, and the turmoil was getting deeper." Occasionally, for the well-being of both pastor and congregation, a change after a brief tenure is sometimes best.

But colleagues who have stayed through difficult circumstances to *tough it out* have often reaped the benefits of their endurance. As one friend explained, "I had the conviction that God wanted us to plant a church here. At the six-month period, I was ready to quit; after three years, we had only thirty people; but now after nine years we have nine hundred." He further related, "For two years, I took every opportunity to contact potential members, but nothing paid off. But in the third and fourth year, everything paid off—all the previous contacts became productive." Similar experiences of other colleagues confirm the value of long-enduring tenures of service.

Jesus said, "My sheep listen to my voice; I know them, and they follow me" (John 10:27). Shepherding requires relationship, and relationships require time for development. The longer we stay at a church, the better people understand our motives and accept our failures. One pastor told me, "One of the benefits of longevity is that when you blow it, fewer and fewer people are shocked; you've just proven you're human once again." Pastors who leave in less than six years are robbing themselves of the fruit of their labors.

Some stay too long, however. A district executive minister observed, "Very few pastors are wired to go beyond eight, nine or ten years in the particular times in which we live." Another likewise lamented, "I constantly see pastors who have stayed two years too long; both they and the church would have been better off if they left earlier." While multidecadal pastorates are not uncommon, the average minister experiences difficulty maintaining the intensity, creativity, and vision necessary for long-term effectiveness in the same setting.

When a new opportunity presents itself, an easy signal to check is the length of your present tenure. Pastors with less than seven years in their church, especially those who have served less than four years, might realize additional fruit if they remain. However, the minister who has reaped the results of seven to ten years of planting is now free to cultivate a new harvest elsewhere.

Strength of Primary Relationships

The signal of primary relationships moves beyond general congregational fit and examines compatibility with key staff and lay leaders. God questioned through the prophet Amos, "Do two walk together unless they have agreed to do so?" (Amos 3:3). Obviously, ministry advancement requires harmony among those guiding the church. Successful service is rarely found where internal conflict divides the leadership.

Areas where tensions have arisen among staff or key lay leaders include the following:

- The initiation and approval of programs
- The hiring of associate ministers
- The expenditure of resources
- The duties and effectiveness of particular workers
- The financing of missions
- The nature of youth ministry
- The decentralization of programming
- The amount of visitation accomplished by the staff
- The style of worship

Effective ministry rarely occurs amid strained primary relationships. So if tensions are irresolvable, the impasse may necessitate a move on the part of at least one party. This was the conclusion drawn by a counselor asked to arbitrate a long-term staff disagreement. Because *differences in philosophy of ministry, style of leadership, and personality are not reconcilable*, he recommended the church negotiate the resignation of one of the associate pastors.

A pulpit committee frequently selects a candidate because they are impressed with the ministry developed in a previous church. Unfortunately, differences in church dynamics may strain their comfort zones once some of those same programs are tried in their own congregation. Adjustment of people to pastor does not happen overnight. Patience and understanding on the part of both parties is necessary. But, as one pastor put it, "If, after five years, you're still questioning the compatibility factor—'Do I respect these people and where they want to go?'—it's time to consider a move."

Whether the primary leaders are the staff, the board, or a combination, harmony of people, purpose, and programs is essential for effective ministry. A high level of compatibility on these elements suggests that you continue serving within this generally wholesome environment. But ongoing tension with the key leaders may be a green light inviting you to transition to a more harmonious field of service.

Credibility Level

"Now it is required that those who have been given a trust must prove faithful" (1 Cor. 4:2). A pastor with established credibility can accomplish great things with a congregation. Conversely, a minister who is suspect among the flock will struggle. Therefore, your degree of credibility with parishioners is another signal worth reading when considering a possible transition.

Most congregants have a basic trust of their pastor, even when they've been disappointed before. Open communication, visible caring, and attention to things that the members deem important builds trust. A pastor's challenge is to take the credibility that he or she has inherited or earned and deepen it even further.

When personal integrity erodes, however, pastors lose their influence with the flock. Chronic self-destructive behavior diminishes one's leadership capability. Credibility busters include the following:

- Defensiveness
- Inability to handle criticism
- Poor decisions
- Not following through on responsibilities
- Not managing conflicts skillfully
- Running a business on the side
- Firing the church organist or secretary (big-time problem in a small church)
- Preaching *you* rather than *we*
- Making major changes in the worship format without adequate preparation
- Inappropriate moral behavior
- Telling several different versions of "the facts"
- Winging it (lack of preparedness)
- Missing significant events, such as funerals or anniversaries

Since we all make mistakes, how do we know when loss of trust is irreparable? Should we stick around and try to repair the damage, or just cut our losses and move on? One colleague made the following observation:

> If you've built mistrust, you have to stop to deal with the cause and reestablish trust. Occasionally, those who have made a significant initial blunder learn through it, and people see that they have a teachable spirit—but more often, in my observation, people don't really recover from this mistrust. Some [pastors] may stay a little longer, spinning their wheels. They eventually find their way out the back door to another ministry or even out of church work.[3]

Quantifying the situation more precisely, another colleague states,

> Sociologists who have studied the viability of groups suggest that, when the number of active congregational members who have lost confidence in their pastor goes beyond twenty-five percent, the critical point has been reached. If conscious efforts do not retrieve a lost confidence, it is wiser for the sake of the viability of the group, to give someone else the opportunity to heal the breach. Once the group is split 50–50, or near this percentage, the danger of power struggles is exceedingly great. Therefore the pastor should be ready for the sake of the group to consider himself expendable long before things deteriorate to this point.[4]

A reputation for high integrity is a good reason for a pastor to continue serving the current congregation. As one minister reasoned, "It would take a long time in a new church to earn the respect I have presently obtained." But the pastor who senses low credibility cannot help but consider transition. We grow through mistakes, and a new congregation can offer a fresh start. Whatever its source, lack of trust is a go-ahead to pursue another call.

Degree of Unity and Support

Another way to assess the pastor/people relationship is to consider the conflicts existing in the congregation. Now tension itself is not bad. A certain amount of tension is needed for good performance, whether in a fishing rod, a sewing machine, our muscles, or a congregation. But if too much tension exists, a line snaps, the thread jams, muscles cramp, or a church becomes dysfunctional. Although congregational disgruntlement leads to resistance, basic harmony fosters joy, encouragement, and growth for both shepherd and flock.

One pastor, reflecting on his long tenure, attributed it to "outstanding treatment by the governing board, expressed through personal support and love." The harmony within that congregation made him want to stay forever.

Unfortunately, this type of unity and support is absent in other churches. Another minister explained how an "internal crisis developed because a group of people was forcing an issue onto the church. The issue was finally settled, but the emotional energy that was expended made me question whether I could remain in this church over the long haul." This associate sensed a need for a change, and later that year made a transition.

Reading this signal accurately requires assessing the depth of any existent discontent. "Many times a pastor will think he has terrific opposition and just cannot stay on as pastor. When he actually finds out how many people are against him, he is amazed to discover that the opposition is not nearly as strong as he thought."[5] On the other hand, a *silent majority* may be very upset but simply remain quiet.

Jesus said, "If a house is divided against itself, that house cannot stand" (Mark 3:25). Chronic conflict or resistance is a signal to move your leadership energy to a more fruitful place of service. But high congregational unity and support flashes a red light and suggests that you enjoy ministry right where you are.

Pastoral Evaluation

When considering a transition, we are basically asking, "Should I stay or leave?" The signal of pastoral evaluation can reveal how those under your ministry would answer the question. Pastors are admonished, "Be diligent in these matters [preaching and teaching]; . . . watch your life and doctrine closely" (1 Tim. 4:15–16). And a pastor's self-evaluation is enhanced and objectified by the observations of those he or she serves.

People judge their pastors regularly. Although they may not use psychometric instrumentation, their comments, both positive and negative, reveal their assessment of our performance. While these informal evaluations are of limited value, a formal evaluation by the church's leadership can provide a legitimate, comprehensive appraisal of how effectively we are serving the congregation.

Annual reviews are not necessarily easy or pleasant. A good evaluation requires time to amass data and then wisdom in communicating the findings. Many lay people are uncomfortable just discussing the strengths and weaknesses of their pastor, let alone suggesting areas for improvement. Ministers are likewise uneasy hearing how congregants evaluate their service.

Pastors may have a dozen or more responsibilities listed in their job descriptions. An annual assessment can help reveal which of those items the board deems most important. For example, if the leadership places high priority on regular visitation, and you commit an abundant time to visiting people, you will likely receive high marks in that area. Contrariwise, if they expect you to be readily available for counseling, but you're seldom free to meet with troubled members, you'll probably receive a lower mark here.

A pastoral evaluation by a church board, however, can also serve as a review of the board's values. In the words of one pastor, "I look forward to my annual review because it's a two-way mirror. It gives me a view of where the leadership is in their priorities." An astute pastor can use this information when weighing the benefits of remaining or leaving.

If the review reveals that the leadership values what you value—in other words, if they affirm your ministry—you have good reason to stay. But if the comments are mainly critical, revealing that the congregation's priorities are considerably different from yours, that's a green light for change. Perhaps with time you could demonstrate the value of your ministry direction, but I tend to agree with the pastor who said, "It's worth considering a move when you can't see the church changing."

Advisors' Counsel

Since decisions are vulnerable to selective perception, we pastors are safeguarded by remembering that "plans fail for lack of counsel, but with many advisers they succeed" (Prov. 15:22). One colleague applied that warning thus: "Each pastor needs a confidant, a mentor, to talk about whether it's time to leave. I need the counsel of others so as not to be stranded with my own decision." The signal of advisers' counsel can provide objective guidance in our decision making.

Some pastors emphasize the importance of receiving counsel from their spouse. One of them said, "The person who understands me the most and has my best interest at heart is my wife. She's my greatest confidant and counselor." Others listened to a trusted friend within the congregation. Many have sought the advice of peers: "A covenant group of friends from seminary days helped me wrestle with my decision." One pastor calls upon denominational executives: "Our district executive has lived with the church longer than I have. I value his opinion." All of these colleagues agree that the magnitude of a decision to resign necessitates collaborative counsel.

Objectivity and honesty are essential qualifications for the advisors we select. It is preferable to choose someone a little distant from the situation or who is at least removed from any emotional investment. This type of objective processing helped one pastor conclude, "As I consulted with several ministry friends, their counsel seemed to be the same. My lack of vision and feelings of burnout were probably an indication that my ministry at this church was coming to a close." His confidence in his decision was strengthened by the collaboration of trusted friends.

When advisors confirm your present ministry through unreserved endorsement, you may view their interpretation as a signal to stay. If, however, they take the risk of questioning your present fit or effectiveness, you should likewise value their counsel. Their input may be the green light that frees you to move toward a more productive ministry.

Summary

Regulatory signals are erected to eliminate ambiguity and give clear guidance. Although they are not posted in the church parking lot, auditorium, or classroom, several congregational signs can give direction to pastors considering transition. Misreading just one sign might not put your life in jeopardy, but you are definitely in danger if you make directional choices against several signs. The seven pastor/ people signals studied in this chapter, along with the congregational and personal signals discussed earlier, can reduce transitional ambiguity. Using the following chart can help you determine whether to stay, go, or exercise caution before making that important decision.

Assessing Your Present Ministry:
Pastor/People Signals

14. Good Sociocultural Fit |__|__|__|__|__|__| Poor Sociocultural Fit

15. Tenure Less than Six Years |__|__|__|__|__|__| Tenure More than Six Years

16. Compatibility with Staff |__|__|__|__|__|__| Poor Staff or Key Relationships

17. High Integrity and Credibility |__|__|__|__|__|__| Low Integrity and Credibility Level

18. Unity and Encouragement |__|__|__|__|__|__| Resistance and Conflict

19. Annual Evaluation Affirms Ministry |__|__|__|__|__|__| Board Requests Major Changes

20. Advisors Confirm Ministry |__|__|__|__|__|__| Advisors Suggest Major Change

6

ASSESSING AN
INVITATION TO MOVE
Congregational Signals

WHAT GOES THROUGH YOUR MIND WHEN you receive a letter from a church that is probing your interest in pursuing a new ministry? Whether your first response is surprise, intrigue, or apprehension, it probably feels good to know that at least *someone* out there knows you're alive. Let's face it, ministry is hard work, and too often our intense labors receive little recognition. Pastors, like parents, are taken for granted. No wonder we feel honored when another congregation wants us!

A contact from a search committee, even at a preliminary stage, suggests, *You're attractive to us, and we're interested in you.* Their letter usually means, *Someone we respect appreciates your ministry enough to recommend you to us, or we think you're the type of minister who could help us.*

Pastors are not in the ministry for strokes, but most of us appreciate knowing that someone recognizes the value of our service. For this reason, a congregational inquiry is very alluring. In addition, the opportunity for a fresh start, a geographical move, or a new flock is more than welcome at times. The pastor who is asking, "Is God behind this inquiry?" needs objective help. Therefore, a careful analysis of the internal health of a calling church can shed light on the wisdom of a move. The congregational signals that one should analyze are self-awareness, self-esteem, pastoral track record, attendance patterns, generosity, and adequacy of resources.

Self-Awareness

Some congregations have clear focus on their overall mission—they understand their identity and core values. One views itself as a Bible-teaching center, another a praise community. One seeks to become a place of fellowship and caring whereas another is a base of operations for social concerns. Still others believe that their *raison d'être* is evangelism. Yet, for every church with a clear purpose statement, hundreds of others lack such specificity. All too frequently, congregations simply do their thing each week, and as long as that thing is sufficiently attended and financed, they keep doing it without knowing why. Stagnation or decline is usually down the road.

Ambiguity of purpose within a congregation leaves the pastor with as many expectations as the church has members. Since no minister can do everything well, his or her efforts are diffused, resulting in limited success and pastoral burnout. Therefore, the more clearly a church can define its uniqueness, the more easily a candidate can determine personal fit. For example, if an inquiring church boasts about its Evangelism Explosion program and attributes its growth over the last decade to that ministry, a prospective pastor can anticipate evangelism expectations from the congregants.

When considering a move, you must acquire certain information about the church's self-awareness early in the candidating process. If the church doesn't provide comprehensive data, request it. Understanding the uniqueness of a congregation is facilitated by asking questions such as the following:

- To whom are you trying to minister?
- What is your church's mission?
- What are your theological and ministry nonnegotiables?
- What are your primary purposes?
- What does your church do really well? Where does it shine?
- How do other churches in town describe your ministry?

- What reasons do new members give for joining?
- How are resources allocated?

If you have to push for clarity or if you get conflicting information, exercise extreme caution. Driving through this intersection may be dangerous. On the other hand, if the congregation's sense of purpose is well defined and its values and goals are compatible with your own, feel free to pursue the relationship further.

Self-Esteem

After receiving a church's self-portrait, you then must ask how they feel about that picture. The signal of self-esteem sheds light on how attractive to members is the image they see in the mirror.

Healthy self-esteem is the product of many variables. Attractiveness of physical facilities is a noticeable factor, but quality of programming and supportive relationships are of greater significance. Positive feelings about the church's overall ministry enhance the marriage of pastor and people. The healthier a congregation's self-image, the more effective will be the pastor's service.

People who visit many different churches notice how greatly congregational self-esteem can vary. You can walk into Church A, for example, and quickly pick up negative vibes. As you participate in worship, attend a Bible class, and talk with the members, you can sense people wondering, *Why are you spending time with us? We're not a very good church.* The members of Church B, on the other hand, exude confidence. It seems as though they are saying, "Before deciding which church to join, why don't you try a few other churches in town. We know you'll be back, but you owe it to yourself to draw that conclusion for yourself."

Healthy self-esteem is exemplified by the congregation whose attitude is, "We have some real areas of strength and also some areas where growth is needed. Nevertheless, we can do all things through Christ who strengthens us." This sense of enjoyment in becoming God's people and doing His kingdom work is contagious. The idea that good preachers make good churches is a myth. The truth of the matter is *good congregations make good preachers*.[1] A church with a healthy self-image motivates its pastor to perform with excellence.

Contrariwise, a negative church can drain the energy of even the most optimistic pastor. This was the experience of one colleague who related, "The congregation I came to was basically unhealthy. I knew the church had some problems with its former pastor and that some feelings were hurt. But I had no idea how badly his ministry had scarred them." Unfortunately, this pastor's service was significantly limited by the congregation's unresolved conflict and its poor self-image.

An unhealthy self-image may also surface as proud complacency. One evening over the dinner table a music minister confided to me, "John, I've led some really great choirs, and I've led some really poor choirs. But this is the only choir I've led that's really poor but thinks it's really great. I can't do anything with them. They think they've got it all together." A congregation with an inflated opinion of itself is as hard to work with as a congregation with low self-esteem.

One denominational leader observed, "If you put a healthy minister into a dysfunctional church, the pastor will become dysfunctional within four months." While a few pastors are specially gifted to move in and heal hurting churches, the average minister will want to avoid a congregation with heavy baggage and a negative self-image. But a calling church that feels good about itself invites further consideration.

Pastoral Track Record

Past performance is the best predictor of future performance. This criterion used by college admissions officers is strongly supported by student research. A similar conclusion can be drawn about ministers and congregations. Just as past ministerial performance is the best predictor of a pastor's future performance, past congregational behavior sheds much light on how that church will function in the future. Because the way a congregation has treated its previous ministers is a good indication of how it will probably treat its next cleric, pastoral track record is definitely a signal worth heeding when journeying toward a new church.

You've probably heard the cliché, "Anyone who follows a founding pastor or a long-tenured pastor will likely end up an interim pastor!" Congregations always need time to adjust to a new minister, especially one whose approach is different. Nevertheless, each vacancy must eventually be filled. Although a congregation may be eager to find a permanent spiritual leader, caution is definitely in order when one is moving toward a church whose previous pastor had a tenure of more than twenty-five years.

An equally difficult situation awaits the pastor whose predecessors served unusually short tenures. Listen to the experience of one colleague: "After I arrived at the church, I learned that they had gone through five associate pastors in the previous seven years. I didn't last long either." Trust levels and credibility are built over time. A succession of short-term ministries weakens a church's ability to follow a new pastor.

Of course, congregational health involves more than having staff people who have worked six to ten years at the church. Nevertheless, respectable tenures do reveal that pastor and people value their relationship. They have gone through the honeymoon bliss and early adjustments of their marriage and have moved into the productive years. A new pastor entering such an environment can anticipate being given sufficient time to develop another ministry chapter in a climate of cooperation.

The best indicator of how receptive a congregation will be to a new pastor's ideas is the way it has treated its previous ministers. Short pastoral tenures in a church's history are red signals; extremely long tenures flash a warning blinker. But reasonable pastoral tenures of six to twelve years shine a green light, a go-ahead to pursue the opportunity.

Attendance Patterns

Attendance is another congregational signal that reflects the health of a church. Since people cast a vote of confidence by their presence, active participation reveals positive feelings about the church's ministry. It follows that growth builds congregational esteem: *Hey, we must be doing something right if all these people are joining!* Growth also facilitates change because a continual influx of new people reduces the power base of resistors. Although dynamic churches inevitably face problems as they grow, the consistent addition of new life is a positive vital sign. Enthusiasm abounds in churches "strengthened in the faith" and growing in membership (Acts 16:5).

During the courtship phase with a congregation, it's important to learn whether the church is growing, has plateaued, or is in decline. Discovering patterns of growth is equally enlightening. You can question, for example, if the church is really stagnant (no change in the numbers of people who attend) or if subtractions through attrition and community demographics are nullifying additions. Has it experienced spurts of growth or a steady increase in attendance? One colleague suggested that a pastoral candidate ask, "To what can these particular periods of growth, or lack thereof, be attributed? What happened at that time in the congregation's life?"

Some churches are located in rapidly growing areas; others see their communities deteriorating. Growth in the former environment is relatively easy, but it is far more difficult in a declining neighborhood. Recognizing the dynamics of a community—including population shifts, economic changes, and the proximity of churches with similar type ministries—tempers the weight of the attendance variable.

Numerical changes caused by internal variables tell a more revealing story about the church. People respond to a caring environment. They gravitate toward good teaching, dynamic worship, and programs that meet their needs. Conclusions about participation and growth should be based primarily on these types of factors because they the are variables over which the church has control.

A growing flock is not the only determinant of whether a move might be productive, but it is one indication of congregational health. Since the signal of attendance patterns quantify the well-being of a calling church, a warning light shines from a church that is experiencing inexplicable decline. Something unhealthful is likely taking place in that congregation. On the other hand, a church that shows regular growth offers the pastoral candidate another reason to view it positively.

Generosity

The well-being of a congregation is also measured by its generosity. Without sufficient finances, ministry effectiveness is limited. The giving practices of church members demonstrate the degree to which they are behind their church. Jesus explained, "Where your treasure is, there your heart will be also" (Matt. 6:21). People vote with not only their attendance but also their checkbooks.

Receiving a copy of the church budget and income record does not in itself provide a pastoral candidate with sufficient information. For example, a church that regularly exceeds its budget may merely be underchallenging its people. On the other hand, a very generous congregation may fall short of its budget when fiscal goals are unrealistically high.

Indebtedness is likewise a tricky variable. Paying out as much as thirty cents on a dollar to service facility debt, for example, hamstrings staff and program development. Overly large indebtedness is a limitation to ministry development. However, congregations that are debt-free simply because they've sold a valuable piece of property or have outlived a mortgage can also be unhealthy.

Generosity is measured in a number of ways, but per capita annual giving is a standard method of comparison. Some church analysts define healthy giving as anything above the national norm. Denominational averages are listed annually in the *Yearbook of American and Canadian Churches* (see fig. 3 at the end of this chapter).[2] A church receiving $1000 per member per year is probably above the national norm whereas a church receiving only $600 per member is on the low side of the giving continuum. But again, any generalization about generosity must be tempered by knowledge of the economic strata of the membership and other local variables.

Another indicator of congregational giving patterns is the apportionment of a budget toward operational overhead as opposed to ministry expenses. Comparing external or missions giving with home-base expenditures reveals a similar statement of priorities. The competitiveness of pastors' salaries likewise tells much about a church (see the national salary survey at the end of chap. 4). Even such small budget items as recognition of staff employment anniversaries and food showers for furloughing missionaries reveal much about generosity.

If a courting congregation is experiencing chronic financial shortages, it is highly appropriate to stop at this red light to investigate underlying causes. However, pastors who sense congregational generosity and fiscal health in a calling church are free to proceed on their journey of exploration.

Adequacy of Resources

Another money-related signal is adequacy of resources. Obviously, strong giving must precede any resource development, but the type of resources into which money flows further reflects a congregation's values and goals. A simple breakdown of church resources includes professional staff, programs and facilities. When trying to determine the color of this "congregational signal," one simply needs to evaluate the configuration and competence of staff, the diversity and effectiveness of programs, and the appropriateness of facilities.

The first place to begin the analysis of a church's staff is to look at the clergy/attendee ratio. Church analysts cite one pastoral staff member for every 125 attendees as the average ratio. Congregations with less than one pastor for every 150 people are understaffed, whereas churches organized for growth usually have at least one staff pastor for every 100 attendees.

Your assessment of staff members should also focus on their specific functions. If the church has a multiple staff, what are the responsibilities of each? How competent are the pastors and important lay leaders? Since the success of a minister in any congregation is largely determined by the overall effectiveness of the ministry team, ask yourself where you would fit. In other words, will your giftedness and philosophy be complemented, duplicated, or hindered by existing staff?

Information about a church's programming is gathered by asking the following questions:

- What types of ministries are provided for families? For singles?
- What strategies are used to draw people into these ministries?
- What is the mix of homogeneous and heterogeneous groupings? (For example, are there intergenerational programs?)
- How adequate are supplies such as teaching materials, choir music, and library resources?

- How do children, youth, and adults feel about the programs designed for their groups?
- What are the staffing ratios in these programs?
- How many programs align themselves for the purposes of worship, education, fellowship, and evangelism? (That is, are all bases covered?)
- How does the church recruit and train volunteers?
- What types of target ministries reach out to the larger community?

Since buildings and grounds exist to support a church's purposes and programs, the adequacy of physical facilities will either enhance or hinder ministry to people. A few starter questions to guide this evaluation include the following:

- Is the size of the auditorium and/or parking lot appropriate? (*Guideline:* used below 80 percent of capacity.)
- Is the educational space sufficient? (*Guideline:* 35 square feet per preschooler, 30 square feet per child and youth, and 25 square feet per adult are good standards for methodologically sound instruction.)
- Are the facilities attractive? (Consider lighting, carpeting, wall coverings, landscaping, and signage.)
- How many hours a week is each building or room used?
- Are there plans to build? If so, what type of facility?

Some churches showcase their elaborate facilities, and some have endowments to subsidize salaries and program costs. Most congregations, however, scramble to stretch their funding across staff, program, and physical plant. Although abundant resources do not guarantee quality ministry, inadequacies in this area most certainly restrict it. Therefore, a church with barely sufficient staff, programs, or facilities emits a negative signal to a pastoral prospect whereas the congregation with resources appropriate to its needs communicates the possibility of productive ministry ahead.

Summary

Before traveling too far toward a new congregation, even before making a campus visit, a pastoral candidate should make an early assessment as to the *health* of a prospective church. The congregational signals of self-awareness, self-esteem, pastoral track record, attendance patterns, generosity, and adequacy of resources provide a wealth of information. For some travelers, the pattern of these lights will suggest abandoning the journey; for others, the composite will encourage further investigation. The following chart will help you rank a calling church on the signals examined in this chapter.

Assessing an Invitation to Move:
Congregational Signals

1. Poor Church Self-Understanding   _|_|_|_|_|_|_|_   Realistic Church Self-Understanding

2. Low Church Self-Esteem   _|_|_|_|_|_|_|_   Healthy Church Self-Esteem

3. Short Pastoral Tenures   _|_|_|_|_|_|_|_   Reasonable Pastoral Tenures

4. Stagnation and Decline   _|_|_|_|_|_|_|_   Vibrancy and Growth

5. Shortage of Finances   _|_|_|_|_|_|_|_   Generous Giving Pattern

6. Inadequate Staff, Program, Facilities   _|_|_|_|_|_|_|_   Adequate Resources

Figure 3

Annual Per Capita Giving
by Selected Denomination

	Inclusive Membership[1]	Per Capita Giving[2]
The Wesleyan Church	123,274	2,058
Evangelical Covenant Church	101,003	1,828
Presbyterian Church in America	306,784	1,626
North American Baptist Conference	49,017	1,237
Seventh-Day Adventist Church	900,985	1,151
Church of the Nazarene	636,564	1,004
Churches of Christ	1,500,000	963
Church of God (Anderson, IN)	234,311	954
Reformed Church in America	285,453	939
Episcopal Church	2,333,327	919
Christian and Missionary Alliance	381,677	851
Presbyterian Church (U.S.A.)	3,455,952	850
Church of the Brethren	134,828	680
The United Church of Christ	1,359,105	627
The United Methodist Church	8,298,145	608
Christian Church (Disciples of Christ)	804,842	604
Southern Baptist Convention	16,052,920	557
General Association of General Baptists	66,296	549
Lutheran Church—Missouri Synod	2,540,045	479
Evangelical Lutheran Church in America	5,099,877	472
American Baptist Church in the U.S.A.	1,442,824	311

1. "Inclusive Membership refers to those with full, communicant or confirmed members plus other members listed as baptized, nonconfirmed, or noncommunicant."
2. These statistics are based on 1998 giving records. Per capita giving is based on inclusive membership. These samples are adapted from the comprehensive *Yearbook of American and Canadian Churches*, 2001.

7

ASSESSING AN
INVITATION TO MOVE
Personal Signals

BECAUSE THE CONGREGATIONAL SIGNALS communicated by a calling church are somewhat quantifiable, they tend to shine distinctly red or green. But personal signals such as giftedness or possible impact are harder to measure. Also, although it's fairly easy to weigh family contentment or job enthusiasm in one's present congregation (see chap. 4), assessment of these concerns is more speculative concerning a not-yet-experienced church. The more information acquired during the courtship phase of a candidating relationship, the more accurate will be one's determination that a ministry marriage is in order.

Giftedness

Pastoral strengths vary as do congregational needs. A minister's gifts and interests can even change over time, just as a church's emphasis will shift at different stages of its life. One colleague described it thus: "The artist uses different sizes of brushes to do various things in his painting. He uses a really broad brush to rough in the sky and other general features, and he uses smaller brushes for the details. I think pastors are like brushes that God uses in creating a masterpiece out of a church. He uses one pastor to accomplish one thing and another to accomplish something else." Effective ministry, therefore, involves being the right person in the right place at the right time.

Reflecting on what we like to do and what we do well gives insight into our giftedness. Testing and feedback from others provide additional input. Over time, we gain a clearer understanding of where we shine and where we struggle. The more accurate a picture we have of ourselves, the easier it is to determine our giftedness fit with a church that expresses interest in securing our service.

Unfortunately, some churches searching for a new shepherd have not delineated a focused pastoral profile. The search process typically begins with a congregational survey, which then translates into a candidate description. These profiles are usually predictable (i.e., good leader, excellent preacher, caring, married, thirty-five to forty-nine, etc.). They may be formulated democratically but not necessarily by the people who have the best read of the congregation.

As a pastoral candidate, you should request both a detailed position description and a prioritization of pastoral functions. More specifically, ask the leadership to quantify the number of hours per week needed for effectiveness in each area. When a clock is superimposed on the functions list, primary requirements will distinguish themselves.

If you have clarified a church's expectations but sense reservations about giftedness fit, consider slowing or curtailing the journey. Continuance is in order only when self-understanding and congregational priorities reflect a similar profile.

Family Interest

Since a pastoral invitation to move is actually directed to an entire family, the input and concurrence of the family is very important. One pastor, not heeding this advice, later lamented, "After living in this town for nine years, I felt the yearning for something different. So I made a unilateral decision and dumped it on my family—and it wasn't a smart move." Another colleague admitted, "One of the major mistakes I made in the transition was not listening to my wife. She had sensed from the very beginning that the new church was not a good match for my gifts and my calling. I knew some of that, but I thought the church would make appropriate changes, which, in fact, it was not able to do."

Most marriages today, even among the clergy, are dual-career relationships. Some ministers' spouses work to supplement a modest pastoral salary; others work to fulfill their own giftedness. The complexity of family life today has led one executive minister to conclude, "Without essential wholehearted agreement that a change is the right thing for all, you'd better not do it." God does not reveal His will only to the cleric.

Children, especially those in adolescence, react with a wide variety of emotions to a possible move. Their first response can vary from *"You* might leave, but we're staying!" to "All right—we're out of here!" A number of pastors in my transitions file warned against moving the family during the teenage years. Others, however, did not rule out making a transition during any stage of their children's lives. One pastor shared a story that illustrates the uniqueness of each situation: "Last year I received an inquiry from a church in California and presented it to my family for their consideration. The girls were vehemently opposed to the move, so we tabled the idea. Strangely enough, we just received another call from Southern California, and this time they're not only interested but excited about the possibility of a move."

The pastor experiencing family resistance to a possible move should slow down to allow time for interest to develop. Additional information on the community may help family members envision what their lives might be like in the new location and adjust to the idea. If opposition persists, it's probably wise to terminate any further communication with the interested congregation. However, even mild curiosity on everyone's part is permission to take the courtship further. And high family interest is a clear signal to pursue the relationship enthusiastically.

Possible Impact

Guess the common denominator across these transitions: a director of Christian education who accepted a senior pastorate; a youth minister who became campus pastor at a Christian college; a senior minister who joined a large church as pastor of adult ministries; and a senior pastor who became a district superintendent in his denomination. In each of these changes, *greater impact* was the chief determining factor.

High impact in my present ministry is the reason one staff pastor continually turns down invitations to the senior pastorate. His mini-congregation of boomers is larger and more active than most churches in his denomination. But another associate minister accepted a senior position because "I would not only have an opportunity to teach the Bible to the whole flock each Sunday but also could set the course of ministry direction. As an associate pastor, I did not have this kind of influence."

Transition to a larger task should not be viewed as an egotistical climb up a career ladder. Rather, it can be an honest petition: "Lord, in your overall game of life, use me wherever I can have the greatest impact for your kingdom." Our desire is to touch lives for Christ, so when an opportunity presents itself to increase our sphere of influence, we must openly consider the possibility.

The signal or impact pushes us to assess the return on our service investment. Upon receiving any letter of inquiry from a church, one colleague questions, "Can I multiply myself more in this new situation?" Another pastor advises, "The minister should investigate very carefully to see if his abilities and strengths will meet the particular need of the church making overtures to him. In other words, do not make a change for change sake, but only when there is advantage to the church, and full utilization of the minister's ability."[1]

Even if you are anxious to move, your present situation may still offer the greater impact. This was the conclusion of one friend who declined a call: "I like new challenges and First Church presented a great opportunity. I wouldn't have agreed to candidate if I were not 95 percent sure that I would have accepted the call if it were offered. But as the candidating week progressed, a knot in my stomach wouldn't go away. I began to feel, 'I don't think you want me here, Lord.' Whenever I thought about the new work, my mind would come back to my present church, and I began to see all that we could do in this ministry right here." Sensing the possibility of greater impact at home, he stayed.

The following questions can help you analyze the impact factor:

- Are fewer people able to do my present job or the prospective job?
- Which situation will demand the best of me? Can I meet those expectations?
- Can I reach a larger number of people through this new ministry opportunity?
- Can I have a deeper influence on the people I touch?
- In which situation will the people most likely multiply my ministry to others?

James reminds us that our life on earth is "a mist that appears for a little while and then vanishes" (4:14). Therefore, we must maximize the moments we invest in kingdom work. If your investigation of a calling church leaves you with reservations regarding impact, remaining in your present ministry may be best for now. But if—after receiving materials from the church and spending time with its leadership—you feel enthusiastic over possibilities, further travel may be in order.

Adequacy of Compensation

One of the most delicate issues to deal with when investigating a new congregation is compensation. Since no pastor should be *a lover of money* (1 Tim. 3:3), it seems unspiritual to probe in the financial area, let alone show displeasure with proposed remuneration. Nevertheless, pastors are responsible for not only the stewardship of their gifts and time but also meeting family and other financial obligations.

For the sake of clarity and fairness, a distinction between pastoral remuneration and congregational expense must be kept in mind. A minister who receives a $65,000 salary, for example, may actually cost the congregation $75,000 annually. Although travel reimbursement, entertainment expenses, insurance premiums, conference fees, and book allowances are not discretionary income, they should be provided by the church. Thoughtful pastors recognize the overall costs that a church bears to support their ministry. Similarly, sensitive congregants realize that a pastor's paycheck is only a portion of the budgeted item called "clergy salary and expenses."

The best way to deal with the compensation issue is to treat it as openly and naturally as any other topic of discussion. Just as you should inquire about a church's history, mission, programs, attendance, and vision, so, too, you should probe into the area of remuneration. Sometimes, predetermined figures have been set by the church board. Other times, salary ranges may be indicated with the specific compensation being open to discussion. Either way, you should know salary parameters before making a decision to candidate.

Professionals who deal with salary negotiations say that it is usually unwise for the interviewee to suggest a salary figure. If we set the figure too low, we may place hardship on our families. If we place the figure too high, we come across as greedy. Besides, if we've never lived in that geographical area, we cannot be sure of contextual dollar values.

If you are asked to put forth a figure, you might respond, "I know what other pastors of churches this size are earning, but I need your help in determining appropriate compensation for this congregation." Let the church be the first to suggest the figure, and then ask what it means in local buying power. One way to get this information is to use a budgeting breakdown to test the reality of individual expense categories. One guideline suggests percentages based on one's net spendable income (after taxes and tithe): housing, 30 percent; auto, 12 percent; food, 12 percent; etc.—see figure 4 at the end of this chapter.[2] One search committee, when asked to follow this procedure, increased their calling package by $2,000. Only after they broke down the proposed figure did they realize that their prospective youth minister couldn't afford housing in their area on 30 percent of the net proposed salary.

If you feel comfortable talking about money matters and can do so in a nonthreatening manner, you will want to inquire about the church's history of salary adjustments. Discussions should move beyond the salary offered at one point in time to the broader philosophy of pastoral compensation. More specifically, you could inquire further by asking, "For what reasons and under what occasions have adjustments been made in remuneration?" Or even, "What has been the church's practice on cost-of-living increases?"

Although pastors cannot expect to get rich from the ministry, neither should they live under financial stress. Although many churches today provide adequate income for their clergy, others are remiss in this area. Caution is in order when a search committee is less than candid about compensation practices. Yet green signals are shining from churches that offer appropriate remuneration and fringe benefits to their pastoral staff.

Proximity to Extended Family

When assessing the pros and cons of a move, proximity to parents and other relatives is another regulating signal. Although this factor might be less significant than giftedness fit, opportunity for impact, or family concurrence, it nevertheless can positively or adversely affect a pastor's personal life and, therefore, his or her effectiveness.

What is the recommended geographical proximity to one's extended family? For newlyweds, a church a thousand miles away might prove to be the healthiest situation. Separation from parents and other relatives can provide time to deepen the new relationship without worrying about in-law expectations. However, a couple with children might prefer closer proximity to family members so that the youngsters can benefit from exposure to godly grandparents, aunts, and uncles.

One colleague related how, after seminary, he and his bride first served a church in the East and eight years later moved to the West Coast. After several years there, part of their openness to a call from a Midwest church was based on proximity to their parents. He explained, "Though we've enjoyed these past fourteen years, this will be the first time we live in the same time zone with our parents. Obviously, this isn't our major reason for pursuing the relationship, but the possibility of just driving to Grammy's house, instead of taking an airplane, is certainly an additional benefit."

Another pastor's concern for extended family affected his decision in a different way, "Accepting the call from the church in California meant we'd have to move far away from both my wife's and my own parents, none of whom are in good health. While we didn't live in the same immediate vicinity, we were able to visit them without taking major vacation time. One of the conditions I made in accepting the call was that I could have a two-week annual study leave. During that time, I would plan my yearly preaching calendar but would do so in the Midwest, where my wife could stay with her parents and I could visit a few times a week."

One by-product of any job relocation may be geographical distancing from our extended family. At various stages of life, we may prefer greater independence or deeper involvement with relatives. If an invitation to move is in the direction of significantly changed family proximity (either closer or farther away), it is wise to stop and consider the implications before making a decision.

Summary

An old verse reminds us, "Only one life, 'twill soon be past; only what's done for Christ will last." Whether you have ten or forty ministry years before you, you will want to live those years with deepest significance.

Recognizing your uniqueness and responding to your giftedness will strengthen your pastoral service. This self-understanding will also help you weigh new ministry opportunities that come your way. Productive ministry changes are rarely accidental. Direction and safety are provided by heeding the personal signals of giftedness fit, family interest, possible impact, adequacy of compensation and proximity to extended family. Use the following chart to assess how these factors would be affected—for better or worse—if you accepted an invitation from a particular calling church.

Assessing an Invitation to Move:
Personal Signals

7. Questionable   _|_|_|_|_|_|_|_   Possible Good
   Giftedness Fit   Giftedness Fit

8. Family Resistance   _|_|_|_|_|_|_|_   High Family Interest

9. Limited Possibilities _|_|_|_|_|_|_|_   High Impact
   or Indecisiveness   Possibilities

10. Inadequate   _|_|_|_|_|_|_|_   Appropriate
    Remuneration   Remuneration

11. Poor Geographical   _|_|_|_|_|_|_|_   Healthy Proximity
    Proximity to   to Extended Family
    Extended Family

Figure 4

Budget Percentage Guide
for Family Income
(Family of Four)

(The Net Spendable percentages are applicable to Head of House-
hold family of three, as well.)[1]

Gross Household Income	$35,000	$45,000	$55,000	$65,000	$85,000	$115,000
1. Tithe	10%	10%	10%	10%	10%	10%
2. Taxes[2]	14.9%	17.9%	19.9%	21.8%	25.8%	28.1%

Net Spendable percentages below add to 100%

Net Spendable Income	26,285	32,445	38,555	44,330	54,570	71,185
3. Housing	36%	32%	30%	30%	30%	29%
4. Food	12%	13%	12%	11%	11%	11%
5. Auto	12%	13%	14%	14%	13%	13%
6. Insurance	5%	5%	5%	5%	5%	5%
7. Debts	5%	5%	5%	5%	5%	5%
8. Entertainment/ Recreation	6%	6%	7%	7%	7%	8%
9. Clothing	5%	5%	6%	6%	7%	7%
10. Savings	5%	5%	5%	5%	5%	5%
11. Medical/Dental	4%	4%	4%	4%	4%	4%
12. Miscellaneous	5%	7%	7%	8%	8%	8%
13. Investments[3]	5%	5%	5%	5%	5%	5%

If you have this expense below, the percentage shown must be deducted from
other budget categories.

14. School/ Child Care[4]	6%	5%	5%	5%	5%	5%
15. Unalloc. Surplus Income[5] —	—	—	—	—	—	—

1. Copyright © 2000, Crown Financial Ministries, Inc., www.crown.org. Used with permission.
2. Guideline percentages for tax category include taxes for Social Security, federal taxes, and a small estimated amount for state taxes based on 2000 rates.
3. This category is used for long-term investment planning, such as college education or retirement.
4. This category is added as a guide only. If you have this expense, the percentage shown must be deducted from other budget categories.
5. This category is used when surplus income is received. This would be kept in the checking account to be used within a few weeks; otherwise, it should be transferred to an allocated category.

8

ASSESSING AN
INVITATION TO MOVE
Pastor/People Signals

MOST OF US CAN REMEMBER GETTING LOST while driving in unfamiliar territory, perhaps on the way to a conference or during vacation. This situation often triggers unproductive behavior. For example, many people admit that they drive faster when they are lost, even when they think that they might be going in the wrong direction!

We don't like uncertainty. Our desire for stability pushes us toward closure. Unfortunately, the dissonance caused by vocational confusion might likewise hurry us in our investigative journeys. But at critical junctions in life, responsible driving requires that we slow down, read the road signs, and seek advice. Speeding up and trying short cuts might only bring us more quickly to a wrong place.

When considering an invitation to move to another church, the signals of mutual awareness, compatibility of background, potential longevity, and advisors' counsel are worthy of study. These pastor/people signals help us assess the potential depth of the new relationship.

Mutual Awareness

Anyone who has studied the decision-making process recognizes the need to begin with the gathering of all relevant facts. Good decisions are impossible in the absence of pertinent data. Because the flow of information between an inquiring church and a prospective pastor is in itself a critical regulatory signal, inadequate knowledge is a red light to stop and investigate each other further.

Mutual awareness requires thoroughness on the part of a search committee and persistence on the part of a pastoral candidate. A competent search committee provides prospective pastors with an accurate picture of the congregation. In turn, it will seek relevant information from each candidate. Although the committee acts as an agent for the church, its composition need not be demographically representative of the congregation. A small group whose members are chosen for their good judgment usually does a credible job of selecting a sound shepherd.

However, since the quality of search committees varies considerably, pastors must also accept responsibility for good knowledge flow if they want to avoid the experience of one colleague who lamented, "I wanted to move, and this looked like an answer to my desire. Regretfully, I didn't ask enough questions up front, so I didn't get enough background information about the church. Shortly after arriving, I realized I wouldn't last long." Critical questioning could have spared his family a lot of pain.

Dislodging the information needed to determine whether a campus visit is in order begins with asking questions of a global nature. The answers to *How . . . ?* or *In what ways . . . ?* provide broad information about the goals and value system of a church. These open-ended questions often uncover issues worth probing through *clarifying* dialogue that fills in the details.

Because probing will sometimes reveal points of tension in a congregation, don't avoid questions that seem to hit a nerve. Sensitive issues are worth knowing about before a marriage! Obviously, the demeanor with which such questions are introduced is important. With a cordial innocence, you could ask, "Are there people in the congregation who view these things differently? If so, what would they say?" Honest, specific questions, when presented in a relaxed, nonthreatening tone, can clarify most ambiguities.

Initial inquiry from a congregation is typically made by phone or letter, with a packet of information sent as a follow-up. After the preliminary contact, however, healthful interaction necessitates deeper verbal dialog.

E-mail is a quick vehicle for communication. Questions can be answered, information exchanged, and arrangements made. Documents can be attached for review. Be careful, however, not to be a pest in inquiring about the status of your candidacy. Due diligence takes time, so expect to hear from the committee only once a month in the early search process.

Many churches use conference calls to communicate with a prospective pastor. When it is used properly, this technology provides an insightful exchange of information, although shoot-from-the-hip conversations may reveal only how well the pastor and committee members think on their feet. More thorough information is obtained when questions are mailed to one another in advance and thought-out responses are given during subsequent phone calls. Clarifying questions can then focus answers on specific issues.

Throughout our marriage, Barbara and I have tried to avoid making impulsive decisions as consumers. Whether the pitch comes from a cookware representative or a health-spa salesperson, if we are pressed to make a decision right now, our default answer is always no. Only after we've studied publicity material, read *Consumer Reports,* and asked advice from friends do we move decisively. Signing a new ministry contract without having adequate information and counsel is even more unwise! If additional information from the church is needed, you had better ask for it. If they still need to know the real you, and you don't keep communications open, an ill-conceived call might be extended—and accepted.

Insufficient knowledge and understanding between yourself and a church signals "Stop! Seek more information." If what you have learned is favorable and you have no unanswered questions, feel free to continue the courtship.

Compatibility of Background

It is much easier to assess pastor/people compatibility in your present ministry than to envision your fit with a calling church. Nevertheless, determining the degree of sociocultural match is important. Thoughtful probing in several key areas can shed light on how harmoniously you will blend with the new congregation.

Regarding the *church's governmental structure,* ask the following questions:

1. What is the relationship of the board (or other governing bodies) to the congregation?
2. What important decisions have been made recently, and at what level in the structure were they determined?
3. What is the work of committees and task forces, and how often do they meet?

Regarding *church practice,* ask the following questions:

1. What style of worship do the congregants prefer?
2. Which programs seem most important to the members?
3. How and by whom are the ordinances/sacraments administered?
4. What annual events are most meaningful to parishioners?

Regarding *lifestyle issues,* ask the following questions:

1. What are the subtle do's and don'ts of the congregation? (For example, how do they feel about the use of alcohol?)
2. Do the members generally agree upon these issues, or is there significant diversity within the church?
3. What sources of entertainment and recreation are available in the church and local community?
4. What type of social activities do congregants prefer?

Personality fit with a new congregation is almost impossible to predict. The best you can do is weigh people's responses to your conversation; therefore, authenticity is critical throughout all interaction. Assessment of overall match is facilitated by maximizing both the amount and the depth of your communication with the congregation.

The *age factor* further influences compatibility. The median decadal age of members tells you if you will be ministering primarily to peers or people a generation away. Pastors who serve parishioners in a life stage similar to their own have a more immediate understanding of what's happening in the lives of their flock.

Another way to look at the life-cycle issue is to consider the age of the previous minister. If a new pastor is more than fifteen years older or younger than a predecessor, he or she is probably a generation removed from the power leadership of the church. This age disparity doesn't necessarily determine pastoral effectiveness, but traditions and comfort zones of the membership are related to age, and they will affect the expectations placed upon the minister.

When a congregation has the opportunity to select a new pastor, it frequently succumbs to the pendulum effect and looks for someone with strengths where the former pastor had weaknesses. What members fail to realize, however, is that they also want to retain the predecessor's strengths. Therefore, the more removed one's *gift mix* is from that of the former pastor, the greater the adjustment needed on the part of a parishioners.

Economic issues provide another window through which you can view compatibility. Is the congregation predominantly white collar or blue collar? What type of cars do most members drive? You should definitely ask, "In which development or neighborhood do you think the pastor should live?" Inappropriate housing choices have damaged many pastoral relationships. Indicators such as style of dress, club memberships or even recreational vehicles provide additional insight into pastor/people match.

Sometimes, incompatibility is recognized early in the investigation. One pastor related, "The inquiry from the church came right at the time when I was open to a possible move, but after an hour-and-a-half conversation with its search committee, I came to the conclusion that who I was, and who they were, simply wouldn't make a good combination." Most often, however, it takes several conversations to get an accurate read.

Whether you reach a conclusion quickly or after much interaction, questionable compatibility is definitely a sign to slow down or stop. But if you sense good chemistry with the church, you are free to proceed through this intersection and move closer toward the new ministry.

Potential Longevity

Since a pastor's credibility is established over time, it's wise to heed the longevity signal when considering a change in ministry, remembering that the most fruitful period of service usually occurs between years six and ten (see chapter 5).

Many search committees ask a candidate to make a ten-year ministry commitment when a call is extended. Most pastors willingly agree, with the disclaimer that if they sense God leading elsewhere, they would have to obey. Nevertheless, an inordinate number of ministers who have agreed to a relatively long-term tenure leave within a few years. Both congregation and prospective pastor should do enough homework to make a realistic longevity commitment based on studied conviction.

Several previously studied signals, when placed in a time context, clarify this issue. A number of questions, including the following, can help you estimate possible tenure in the new church:

1. Do I sense a vision for the church that might take four, seven, or ten years to complete?
2. Will the church need my areas of strength eight years down the road?
3. Will the church enter a new chapter in its life in less than ten years? Can I lead them into that new chapter?
4. From what I know about the church and surrounding community, do I want to invest one-fourth of my ministry career here?
5. Will my family grow through participation in this church and community during the next ten years?
6. Is there something else I'd rather be doing five years from now (denominational work, seminary teaching, etc.)?
7. Do any foreseeable road blocks surface that could stifle future ministry (e.g., limited facilities, land, etc.)?

Fruitful ministry blossoms within the context of personal relationships. The apostle Paul's effectiveness, for example, welled up from an intimacy described as "a mother caring for her little children" (1 Thess. 2:7). Therefore, a warning goes out to the seminarian considering a short-term associate position as a jumping-off point for a senior pastorate, to the minister in an intolerable situation who is ready to move just anywhere, or to any other cleric who is tempted to accept an offer where long-term service is doubtful.

If an eight-year tenure seems unrealistic, from either your viewpoint or the church's, this red light warns you to stop and reconsider the implications of the move. But if a decade of profitable service is foreseeable, the inquiry is worth pursuing.

Advisors' Counsel

Seeking input from others counteracts our susceptibility to selective perception. Again, in the words of Solomon, "Plans fail for lack of counsel, but with many advisers they succeed" (Prov. 15:22). The counsel of trusted friends and colleagues provides additional data at critical junctures of transition.

Sometimes that feedback comes unsolicited. "You know, Bill, every time I've heard you preach, you've delivered a winner. I wouldn't be surprised if someday a church hauls you off to serve as its senior pastor." Accumulated comments of this kind will contribute to your self-understanding and broaden your professional objectives.

On other occasions, more direct counsel is needed. "You know the church well, Harold, and you've observed my ministry for over a decade. Do you think this church and I are right for each other?" The better these advisors know you, and the more information they have on the church, the more helpful will be their guidance.

Of course, widening the circle of knowledge regarding a church inquiry is potentially dangerous. One pastor observed, "Once the word is out that you're looking, or that you've candidated at another church, you're really finished at your present church." Even though this colleague's generalizations aren't cast in concrete, interviewing with another church can erode intimacy and trust with your present congregation. Therefore, the advisors you choose must be able to keep a confidence. Very often, a minister's best confidants are persons outside the congregation, whether a denominational leader, another pastor, or a close friend.

When objective advisors with your best interests at heart tell you that a move looks questionable, heed their warning and slow your journey toward an inquiring congregation. But if people with sound judgment give an affirming nod, perhaps you should seriously consider the move.

Summary

The journey toward another place of service typically involves an exploratory inquiry, an exchange of information, interviews, and, finally, a firm invitation to candidate. A church may send out many letters of inquiry, knowing full well that only one person will be suitable to its needs. Likewise, a pastor may receive many contacts from churches, realizing that a move is not necessary every time a letter arrives. A good ministry marriage is not an accident. Careful assessment of the pastor/people signals outlined on the following page will provide directional guidance.

As with the other criteria by which an invitation to move should be evaluated, one green light doesn't signal an automatic go; the road ahead may still have potholes. Nor does one red light mean that the trip should be canceled. Although the brilliance of these lights will vary for each pastor approaching the signals, a directional pattern will likely emerge. Interpreting that pattern correctly will bring the confirming peace of the Holy Spirit and thereby indicate whether a change is right at this moment.

Assessing an Invitation to Move:
Pastor/People Signals

12. Inadequate Knowledge Flow   _|_|_|_|_|_|_| Comprehensive Knowledge Flow

13. Questionable Background Fit   _|_|_|_|_|_|_| Good Background Fit

14. Eight-Year Tenure Doubtful   _|_|_|_|_|_|_| Eight-Year Tenure Likely

15. Negative Advisor Warning   _|_|_|_|_|_|_| Affirming Advisor Endorsement

9 PASTORAL ASSESSMENT

Next Tuesday evening, Bob will meet with the executive committee of the church board for his annual review. Although past evaluations were generally positive, each year the process has evoked anxiety. This time, however, Bob is actually looking forward to the board's appraisal. A month ago, he received an inquiry from another church, and the new opportunity looks promising. However, Bob doesn't know if he should leave New Covenant, so he's particularly interested at this time in the board's evaluation of his service.

Bob's not the type of person to lay out a fleece, so he is hoping that the upcoming evaluation will signal the advisability of staying or leaving. His present church's assessment of his ministry is a piece of the puzzle that he needs for making a wise decision. If the leadership still values what he values and affirms his ministry, he'll probably stay. But if the congregation's expectations and priorities move away from his dreams and giftedness, Bob is ready to seek another pastorate.

Performance evaluations are standard in many professions, but they are more complicated for clergy. First, congregants may disagree as to pastoral duties and their relative importance. Ministers are expected to preach, lead worship, counsel, visit, evangelize, motivate, develop leadership, administer, teach, and manage conflict. Obviously, not everything can be achieved with equal proficiency. Second, assessing the personality of the minister is very important but more subjective than judging his or her performance. Spiritual passion, concern for others, tact, flexibility, and sincerity are rather hard to measure. Although members may complain about quality of preaching or frequency of visitation, failure in ministry more often can be traced to relational difficulties.

A third complicating factor is that pastors are evaluated by the very people upon which they depend for success. It doesn't seem right that a member can decide not to participate in the ministry of the congregation and then judge a pastor on how well the church is going.

Pastoral assessment is not an easy process. In fact, quite a few of us have had negative experiences in this area! Nevertheless, the benefits of periodic evaluations clearly overshadow their drawbacks.

The Benefits of Performance Reviews

Pastoral assessment provides a channel for people to express their feelings. You've probably heard the expression *roast preacher.* That Sunday menu item is a type of informal assessment. Members make judgments about a church's ministry—and, more particularly, the minister's performance—regularly. Rather than just letting these comments float around in the congregation unanswered, it's wise to set up a means for channeling specific concerns toward resolution. The annual review can serve as such a vehicle.

Pastoral assessment reveals ministry strengths. A good evaluation identifies both strengths and deficiencies. Too often, we hear only the criticism, yet capitalizing on strengths is far more productive. When a church board identifies what is going well, we recognize what, above all else, we should keep doing, and we are encouraged to build on those strengths.

Systematic evaluation reveals growth areas. During one review, a pastor was commended for his teaching, which was organized and easy to follow. He provided the congregation with a balanced content and used methods that drew people into the study. Furthermore, people thought that the materials he provided for them were excellent. However, a theme that came back from several sources was that typically too much content was given for the time allotted per session. The material was being dumped rather than worked through. As a result of this feedback, the pastor was able to rethink his approach and modify the amount of information packaged into his sermons and class sessions.

Formal evaluation allows clarification of expectations. Performance is hard to measure in the absence of criteria, yet the weight of specific items will vary even within a well-written job description. Sometimes only through a systematic evaluation process can the pastor and board realize that they are assigning different values to particular aspects of the ministry. Talking about these differences openly and without being defensive facilitates understanding. For example, explaining the rationale behind a program, or how it fits into overall objectives, is certainly appropriate at evaluation time. After expending a considerable amount of effort gathering data and formulating it into an appraisal, board members desire feedback on their perceptions. Evaluations are not an end in themselves; they are a springboard for discussion and refinement of ministry.

Pastoral assessment is a mirror for congregational fit. If I view preaching as my primary function, and my review also reveals it to be a priority of the leadership, my ministry efforts will seem productive. On the other hand, if I spend significant time with cell groups only to hear that the board thinks that these groups are unimportant, I might seriously question the value of my labor. In preceding chapters, we looked at the personal signals of personality, giftedness, cultural background, dreams, and priorities, and we concluded that these are some of the indicators of pastor/people compatibility. However, determining fit on our own might be shortsighted; therefore, receiving feedback from those under our ministry is vital. An annual appraisal provides the opportunity to interpret those signals from the membership's vantage point.

Some *Don'ts* of Assessment

The usefulness of a pastoral review rests primarily upon the integrity of the process itself. The timing of assessments, the selection of evaluators, and the criteria applied all color the results. Both the minister's self-esteem and the board's leadership are diminished by improper evaluation techniques. Because spiritual growth and mutual assistance are the ultimate goals of a competent evaluation, several assessment pitfalls should be avoided.

Don't seek evaluation amid conflict. Too often, a pastor asks for a performance review when tensions have arisen in the congregation. Likewise, boards frequently press for a review only after problems become serious. By this time, biases are already set in place. The temptation to use the appraisal for self-vindication or a show of power is too high. Little will be accomplished when an atmosphere of discontent is prevalent. Most often, it is the minister who is damaged in the process.

Don't be flattered by a highly positive assessment. All of us have strengths and weaknesses. In fact, every personality trait has a positive side and a negative side. The strongly self-disciplined pastor may struggle with flexibility, the more spontaneous one with staying focused on a task. God, the author of personality and giftedness, has wired each of us to do some things really well. Those particular strengths do not make one person superior to another, only more effective in specific areas. The strengths mentioned by an evaluative team simply identify endowments on which you should capitalize. They do not imply that you are the perfect personification of that ability, merely that your contribution is maximized by using those strengths.

Don't be crushed by criticism. Each of us has enough weaknesses to keep even the most gifted person humble. While it's more polite nowadays to talk about *growth areas* rather than weaknesses, the bottom line is that, in both personality and performance, you have areas in which you do not shine. Therefore, don't be surprised or devastated when you're criticized. One colleague suggests,

> An absence of criticism should not be your goal in ministry, although I admit that criticism is always painful for me. Lack of criticism means one of two things: You are doing such a good job no one can complain, or you've got people intimidated, afraid to speak up. The latter leads to criticism behind your back—a far more dangerous situation than being criticized directly.[1]

Don't be defensive. We understand cognitively that assessment identifies strengths worth unleashing and growth areas that call for improvement. Emotionally, however, most of us still struggle when our weaknesses are spotlighted. Sometimes we become overly defensive when people devalue what we perceive as strength. We may also react hostilely when the critic identifies a concern that we know is a weakness but that we have trouble admitting to ourselves. For some people, defensiveness leads to emotional diatribes; for others, arms fold, legs cross, and withdrawal sets in. Neither response is healthy. Defensive denial impedes growth; gracious acceptance and further analysis usually prove beneficial to pastor and people alike.

Don't talk too much. One minister states, "I don't talk when the board makes its evaluation. I'm there to listen. I may ask questions for clarification, but the time is for their feedback, not for me to defend what I do." Generally, I agree with this colleague. We have many other occasions for preaching, teaching, and instruction, but the evaluation is primarily a time for listening. Nevertheless, communication is enhanced by your asking questions, seeking clarification, and probing for meaning. A dignified verbal exchange relaxes the atmosphere of a potentially tense situation. Although too much speech on our part signals that we really don't want to hear what is being said, clamming up may be read as a passive-aggressiveness, which is equally nonproductive. A modest amount of response is beneficial to healthy interaction and thereby is a catalyst for optimal growth through the assessment process.

Don't tie evaluations to merit pay. Congregations vary in how they establish clergy compensation. One church sets salary in light of the degree of supervisory responsibilities. Others relate remuneration to years in the ministry, educational attainment, or length of service. Some churches match salaries with those of other professions (e.g., teachers or school principals). Some churches try to keep salaries competitive with the salaries offered by congregations of comparable size. Since many factors relate to contextually adequate remuneration, tying evaluation to salary adjustments is problematic.

Linking salary to a board review transfers the ownership of the assessment to the board, encouraging a pastor-as-employee mentality.

Furthermore, how much of a raise is good preaching worth? Should a pastor's salary be adjusted if the church has moved to double services? Should compensation be adjusted because the church has hired a part-time associate? Pastoral evaluations accomplish their purpose best when they are not related to compensation.

The *Do's* of Assessment

We are helped in the evaluation process when we keep the big picture before us. Although the most valuable assessment of your performance may be your own, you are there to receive objective feedback on how you are doing. You have not initiated the process to renegotiate compensation, nor have you drawn together the leadership for a time of instruction. You have asked these observers to assess your strengths and growth areas, so pride or defensiveness is inappropriate. You are simply present to hear their report. The negatives to guard against during evaluation are best kept in check by practicing specific do's of assessment.

Do start the process early. Car mechanics tell us that it's more cost effective to perform routine maintenance than to repair major engine problems caused by neglect. Just as dentists would also rather practice prevention than to install crowns, systematic feedback on ministry effectiveness proves less costly than waiting until problems mushroom in the congregation.

Many pastors ask to have an initial evaluation after six months with the new congregation, with subsequent reviews every twelve months. Since your first contact with the church was probably through the search committee, you might suggest that the first review team include members of that group. They were the people who formulated the job description, presented a portrait of the congregation, and relayed its expectations, so their participation is helpful if a misunderstanding arises.

Do encourage regular assessments. When things are going well, no one at the church will want to spend time on performance reviews. But when a crisis surfaces, some people react by wanting to fix blame on their pastor. Conducting an evaluation at such a time is rarely profitable. Annual reviews minimize the prejudicial effect of a conflict situation.

An objective review board seeks input from as many people as possible and traces long-term performance across all pastoral functions. One colleague expressed it thus: "The questionnaire really lets me see how others view me. Since this review process is an annual occurrence, I'm motivated to keep growing and improving as a person and as a pastor. The key is knowing I'm being held accountable by people interested in my growth."[2] Fine tuning ministry direction when things are running smoothly is a lot easier than making radical changes in response to trouble. For this reason, suggest setting an annual date for the review process.

Do claim ownership of the evaluation. A big difference exists between a board-dominated review and an assessment in which the pastor can participate. Often, board members are executives in the corporate world who assume that the church can be run like a business. Few people understand the complexity of volunteerism as it relates to the accomplishment of ministry goals. Evaluations used as a club by the lay leadership never generate the growth achieved by clergy-owned assessments.

A good board wants to provide a minister with regular, honest feedback, but wise pastors take the initiative in defining how that process will take place. The starting point is for you to establish a time frame for the review and see that an evaluation committee is selected. This should not be a group of yes men (or yes women) but three to four individuals who understand the mission of the church, its goals and objectives, and the agreed-upon expectations for you, its spiritual leader. If you have a high regard for these people, it will be easier to accept their findings. After interacting with this smaller group, you can use their feedback to reshape your ministry directions and personal efforts.

Do accept the perceptions of evaluators. Although you might disagree with an individual's assessment of your performance, remember that people's feelings and impressions are real to them. Responding, *That just isn't so!* attacks the person. Disparaging an opinion suggests that this person is incapable of making evaluations. It is best at this stage just to listen and later test the validity of any negative comments.

One colleague shared this story:

> My first time through this process, I was confused and a
> little hurt by answers to one question about leadership.
> While many saw me as very adequate, others did not. I asked
> for some clarification and found out that those who worked
> with me on a daily basis around the office and in ministry
> saw my leadership in a positive light, while several on the
> board did not.
>
> I was jolted. I didn't think any member still had the 'just
> a youth pastor' mentality. Was I still being judged accord-
> ing to this view, even after thirteen years of experience?
> Immediately I began plotting how to increase my leader-
> ship perception from the board level. Should I wear a suit
> to the meetings? Speak more often? More forcibly? Should
> I take board members to expensive lunches? The Holy Spirit
> quickly showed me how immature and ludicrous those
> thoughts were. Neither the kingdom's advancement nor
> my calling to love teenagers would be served by childish
> efforts to make people think I was a leader. I had to learn
> (again) that I am perceived differently by different sets of
> people. To some I am just a youth pastor. I suppose as long
> as I'm in youth ministry I will confront this attitude and
> have to cope with my own internal reaction to it.[3]

Disagreeing with someone doesn't mean that we have to prove them
wrong. A cordial, accepting demeanor goes further than contentious-
ness in changing a critic's view.

Do press for objective feedback. Structured assessments encourage objectivity. Unguided processes create problems and misunderstandings. One
author has commented, "The informal, casual evaluation of clergy is
often individualistic, removed from the context of the church. This
kind of evaluation reduces to appearances and demeanor. People like—
or do not like—the way they talk, look, or act. The casual expertise in
evaluating clergy is often based on personal likes and dislikes."[4]

This type of subjective assessment is further biased by the personal turmoil that people may be experiencing. "Severe criticism of a particular pastor arises from the frustrations of the critic. The internal soul of the critic is hurting and he or she projects his or her feelings outward, on the pastor. The critic may be experiencing a personal loss, or the death of a loved one, the death of a community known and loved for years, the death of a beloved church. The basis of such criticism, then, is internal, not external."[5]

While selective perception cannot be eliminated on the part of your reviewers, interpretive bias can be minimized through the use of forms and procedures for the assessment. Rather than just asking, "How is pastor doing?" specific points of a job description can be reviewed. Instead of allowing a free-for-all on high times and low moments in clergy demeanor and performance, ask that specific character qualities and ministry competencies be measured.

A deacon once asked me, "John, Pastor Dennis would like an evaluation. How do we go about it?"

I answered, "Simply take your agreed-upon expectations, carefully solicit feedback from people who understand the ministry, and then share it with Dennis."

His response was, "We don't have a job description, so expectations haven't been defined."

I replied, "Then it's difficult to conduct a fair appraisal. For now, you're better off developing performance expectations, then reconvening in six months to measure progress."

A concise and objective way to denote progress is for the church to develop a list of "commendations and recommendations" for each responsibility in your job description. Since the purpose of assessment is growth, recommendations for improvement should be reasonable, not overwhelming. One recommendation per area of responsibility will identify enough growth areas to address during the coming year. A summary report might look something like this:

Preaching
Commendations
- Good overall planning; balance in Scripture selection

- Evidence of adequate preparation and investment of time
- Good sensitivity toward needs within the congregation

Recommendation

- Focus the application; sometimes too shotgunned

Staff Supervision and Administration

Commendations

- Evidence that staff is maturing and working together closely
- Secretarial work is accomplished in a timely and effective fashion
- Good cooperation between CE personnel and school personnel

Recommendation

- Initiate annual evaluations for support staff

Visitation

Commendations

- A consistent, coordinated effort by the pastoral staff provides visitation and follow-up for hospitalized and shut-ins
- Personal calls to visitors and follow-up for assimilation are practiced routinely
- Maintains good supervision of adult class leaders regarding needs within the care groups

Recommendation

- Develop greater accountability of adult class leaders regarding assimilation of seekers

Commendations delineated in the review should focus on what's going right with your ministry, what you don't want to lose. Recommendations reflect areas that need strengthening. Since ministry gains are best made by capitalizing on strengths, receiving a generous list of commendations is highly motivational. Identifying just one growth area per expectation usually total eight to ten specific suggestions for development, more than enough for the coming year!

Another tool used by churches to achieve review objectivity is the appraisal survey. Questionnaires are distributed to people familiar with a pastor's or staff person's ministry, and the respondents are asked to evaluate performance in several areas. For example:

- Provides spiritual leadership for those under care
- Is fair in dealing with people during conflict situations
- Provides clear and consistent directions
- Gives people freedom within their proper sphere to do God's work in their own style
- Is accessible when needed
- Keeps his/her word on commitments; is faithful
- Is an example of high moral and ethical character
- Counsels people facing major life decisions (such as marriage)
- Maintains a trust level between pastor and congregation of sufficient depth and breadth to constitute an effective partnership

While subjective judgments are called for by the individuals completing the questionnaire, averaging the results lends objectivity to the evaluation process. Forms for such appraisals are readily available, but many churches have developed their own instruments from the most applicable points in surveys used elsewhere. A sample form is located at the end of the chapter (see fig. 5).

Do reprocess the evaluation after a "cool down." The session during which the evaluative team shares its results is primarily a time for you to listen. The men and women who have volunteered to strengthen your ministry through evaluative feedback may not be experts. Even if you do not like the way they express some things or you disagree with their findings, for the well-being of the evaluative team—and your professional growth—it's best to guard against knee-jerk reactions. One pastor shared this story:

> Recently a fellow handed me a letter with several points of criticism. Most of them I can handle, but the final point hit me at the wrong time, and the way it was phrased hit one of my own sore points, an area where I had been painfully attacked before. I reacted sharply—"I'm with you

through point five, but when you hit point six, you don't know what you are talking about!" Later, after talking it over with an associate, I realized the critic somewhat innocently hit my emotional flash point. So when weighing criticism, it is important to ask, "Is this touching an area that's emotional nitroglycerin for me?" If so, I need to be extra careful and rely on the judgments of trusted friends.[6]

Reviewing an appraisal a couple of days later can help you study the feedback more objectively. The cooling-down period might not change your feelings about some of the assessments, but you will probably be better able to accept the findings as real to the evaluators and can then move on to develop next year's professional-development program.

The Big Picture

Several of my friends have this motto in their office: *"The main thing is to keep the main thing the main thing."* When considering assessment, remember that forms are important, ownership is significant; a supportive, objective evaluation team is critical; and a mature response is essential. But amid these particulars, don't lose sight of the big picture: evaluation is designed primarily for refining directions. Whether you are presently comfortable in your church or sense that you are approaching an intersection of transition, pastoral assessment can provide objective, systematic feedback for measuring your ministry effectiveness and fit.

Figure 5

Annual Performance Appraisal
Appraisal Questionnaire

This form is condensed from one used at North Seattle Alliance Church.[1] The full form as used by the church is spread over several pages to provide space for written comments in addition to the numerical ratings.

Person completing form:
☐ Governing Board   ☐ Pastoral Staff   ☐ Support Staff   ☐ Other

Annual Performance Appraisal for: _____

The following questions identify some of the numerous factors that make for an effective pastoral staff member. The person being evaluated is interested in improving ministry to people.

This form is being completed by several persons. Your ratings will be grouped with others, and only composite results will be seen by the person being evaluated. The composite will also be reviewed by the personnel committee of the Governing Board, with results reported to the full board.

Please do not sign this form. You may return it in the envelope provided. If it is not returned within two weeks, it will be assumed you do not wish to participate.

Date Completed: _____

      I know this person very little: _____ (Return questionnaire
                                                    unanswered.)
      I know this person somewhat: _____
      I know this person well: _____
      I know this person very well: _____

---

1. Used by permission of North Seattle Alliance Church, Seattle, Washington.

Public impression (circle any applicable description and comment if you wish):

General Appearance	**Voice**	**Posture**	**Facial Expression**
Neat	Too fast	Stiff	Accepting
Sloppy	Too slow	Athletic	Severe
Good taste	Good variety	Slumped	Dignified
Poor taste	Good diction	Loose-limbed	Serious
Striking	Poor diction	Controlled	Happy
Average	Monotonous	Erect	Unhappy

Please rate as many as possible of the following items, using this scale.

1   Superior, outstanding.
2   Good, above average
3   Average, adequate, could be strengthened.
4   Poor, inadequate, needs much strengthening
N/A   Not applicable or insufficient knowledge for rating.

	1	2	3	4	N/A
1. Provides spiritual leadership for those who look to him/her.	—	—	—	—	—
2. Has rapport with those with whom he/she works.	—	—	—	—	—
3. Is positive and equitable in relationships with other staff members.	—	—	—	—	—
4. Is sensitive to the varied needs of people at all levels of experience and background.	—	—	—	—	—
5. Is open to input from others in recommending and maintaining reasonable standards.	—	—	—	—	—

6. Is fair in dealing with people in conflict situations.   —   —   —   —   —

7. Avoids exchange of derogatory remarks with others.   —   —   —   —   —

8. Helps people set and achieve meaningful goals.   —   —   —   —   —

9. Lets me know when I do a good job.   —   —   —   —   —

10. Encourages me to try new methods and approaches in my work for Christ.   —   —   —   —   —

11. Seems to keep a proper balance between his/her church work and family time.   —   —   —   —   —

12. Provides clear and consistent directions.   —   —   —   —   —

13. Does not make unreasonable demands on my time.   —   —   —   —   —

14. Respects and seeks to know my individual characteristics, talents, and potentials.   —   —   —   —   —

15. Treats me as a responsible person.   —   —   —   —   —

16. Gives people freedom within their proper sphere to do God's work in their own style.   —   —   —   —   —

17. Evaluates me fairly, both formally and informally.   —   —   —   —   —

18. Has the ability and courage to give constructive criticism in a friendly, firm, and positive manner.   —   —   —   —   —

19. Is hospitable to my opinions, whether solicited or volunteered, and considers them fairly without prejudice.   —   —   —   —   —

20. Openly accepts suggestions and implements them where workable.   —   —   —   —   —

21. Anticipates problems.   —   —   —   —   —

22. Is accessible when needed.   —   —   —   —   —

23. Is a *team player,* not a *lone ranger.*   —   —   —   —   —

24. Seems to work by established priorities.   —   —   —   —   —

25. Seems not to be overwhelmed by a volume of lesser tasks.   —   —   —   —   —

26. Is perceived to be fully committed to NSA, its people, and purposes.   —   —   —   —   —

27. Is approachable; I would gladly seek his/her help in solving a personal problem.   —   —   —   —   —

28. Seems knowledgeable and competent in his/her area of ministry.   —   —   —   —   —

29. Does not display impatience/ irritation with people and programs that might be delaying progress.   —   —   —   —   —

30. Keeps his/her word on commitments; is faithful.   —   —   —   —   —

Please complete if you have had adequate opportunity to observe the individual's preaching ministry:

31. Presents ideas clearly and understandably.   —   —   —   —   —

32. Makes Scripture applicable to my life.   —   —   —   —   —

33. Seems to enjoy preaching.   —   —   —   —   —

Please complete if you have had adequate opportunity to observe the individual's teaching ministry (Wednesday prayer meeting, small-group Bible study, etc.):

34. Presents ideas clearly and understandably.   __   __   __   __   __

35. Encourages discussion.   __   __   __   __   __

36. Keeps things on track without being rigid or inflexible.   __   __   __   __   __

37. Handles distractions and/or discipline.   __   __   __   __   __

38. Makes material applicable to my life.   __   __   __   __   __

39. Seems to enjoy teaching.   __   __   __   __   __

40. Demonstrates overall competence and organization.   __   __   __   __   __

41. I have confidence in him/her.   __   __   __   __   __

42. I have respect for and confidence in his/her judgment.   __   __   __   __   __

Thank you for your investment of time and interest in this individual's ministry!

10

THE CANDIDATING PROCESS

THE PROCESS OF BECOMING PASTOR to a congregation is similar to the steps leading up to marriage. At one end of the personal relationship continuum is the becoming acquainted stage; at the other end lies deep awareness and intimacy. The process moves from dating, to going steady, to engagement, to the wedding ceremony, in which the exchanging of vows seals the relationship before God and state.

As a dating couple spends time together and enjoys each other's company more and more, their relationship grows and their thoughts turn to making their relationship permanent. Their chances for a successful marriage, however, depend on the *quality* of their courtship. A rocky dating relationship is seldom followed by a stable marriage, but a courtship characterized by honesty and discovery usually results in a healthy, long-term commitment.

The making of a strong ministry marriage likewise requires relational wisdom. Authenticity and transparency are required of both prospective pastor and congregation. As subsequent conversations deepen knowledge and understanding of one another, they reach the *going steady period,* during which little time and energy are given to any other relationships. Eventually, the church may *pop the big question,* leading to an engagement period called *candidacy.* The marriage of pastor to new congregation is confirmed when both parties say *I do* after the official candidating visit.

Dating: Getting Acquainted

On our first date, Barb and I attended a late-evening movie; on our second date, we attended an Easter sunrise service. Subsequent opportunities to get better acquainted included dinners, school events, carnivals, picnics, sporting events, plays, and numerous church activities. Our relationship developed by being together. It was only later, when Barbara went to college, that writing became our primary mode of communication.

The dating game with pastor and courting congregation, however, almost always begins with a written exchange of information. Before getting serious, both parties need to get to know each other better. The types of material useful for becoming acquainted include the following:

A mission or purpose statement. What is this church's reason for existing? Are members clear on what they want to accomplish? Have they intentionally thought about ministry direction? A marriage between church and pastor is hard to envision if the congregation is unable to articulate its own goals and objectives. Predicting harmony is much easier when the congregation has worked out its mission and directional thrust for the future.

A self-study or consultant's report. During a pulpit vacancy, many churches survey their members and analyze their ministry. They may either conduct a self-analysis or use an outside resource to help them develop their profile. Reviewing a copy of a self-study can expand a prospective candidate's understanding, and a consultant's report can provide additional objective data.

Pastoral profile and job description. Although commonality exists among pastoral roles, congregations vary on how they weigh specific functions. For this reason, a pastoral profile and job description are essential during the acquaintanceship stage. Is the church looking for primarily a shepherd or an equipper, a generalist or a specialist, a lover or an administrative leader? What proportion of time should be directed toward leadership development, preaching, and care giving? Contextual variables (size, location, ethnic mix, etc.) temper pastoral priorities.

Doctrinal statement, covenant, affirmations. Obtaining documentation on a church's beliefs and official positions is necessary, even when the minister and the inquiring church are within the same denomination. Congregations rarely experience tension over major doctrines, but battle lines have been drawn over the role of women, the relevancy of charismatic gifts, having divorced persons in leadership, and a number of social justice issues. If the materials from a church do not include statements about such items, requesting them is most appropriate. An early reading on the climate of the church is sometimes possible through these documents.

A history of the church. Most congregations include a historical sketch in the packet of materials sent to pastoral prospects. The history gives the chronological overview of how the church became what it is today. Information selected for inclusion in the history provides insight into what the members prize most highly.

Community demographics. Although some churches provide a detailed study on surrounding neighborhoods, others offer only a general guesstimate. Obviously, the more information a prospect has on age groups, ethnic mix, economic stratification, population densities, traffic patterns, zoning and housing, and employment opportunities in the area, the easier it is to envision ministry possibilities.

Attendance patterns. Statistics on membership totals and attendance for the last ten years are worth requesting if the church has not already provided them. Membership numbers are useful if the method for inclusion is noted, but actual participation in Sunday school, morning worship, and other programs is of greater benefit. A pastoral candidate's picture of the church is further enhanced by knowing both the median age (mathematical average) and the modal age (largest cluster group) of the parishioners.

A budget history. What is the church's average per capita giving? What patterns and trends emerge? How much debt has been encumbered? What percentage of the budget finances that debt? How generous is funding for missions? What other fixed expenses are noted? Since most churches will query candidates on their management of personal finances, requesting a ten-year financial overview is fair turnabout on the minister's part.

Governance structure. Information about a church's method of governing is usually found in its constitution. Procedures for holding office or conducting business are typically delineated. However, although the document usually describes lines of accountability, it rarely details parameters of pastoral authority. Yet, a candidate should know whether he or she can invite a guest to fill the pulpit, for example, or if that would need board approval. The better a prospective pastor understands the church's governance procedures, the clearer he or she can envision potential harmony.

A description of programming for children, youth, and adults. What does church look like to the average attender? What new programs have been added in the last two years? How centralized or decentralized are the various ministries? Do special emphases and related curricula flow from the church's overall mission? The life of any church goes beyond history, statistics, and community demographics. The focused activity of the congregants tells us much about life within the parish.

A description of facilities. Since the activities in a church are closely linked to the nature of its campus, a description of the physical property provides a context for understanding statistics and program. The seating capacity of the auditorium, square footage of classrooms, and amount of on-site parking are basic information. The age and condition of buildings is also important to discuss. Weekday use of space gives further detail to one's mental picture of the church's functioning.

Anticipated changes and plans. Knowing a church's past and present is essential. But what does the congregation envision for the future? Does the church anticipate any renovations or expansion projects on their present site? Are the lay leaders considering relocation? Do they have a desire to plant a mission church? Before a pastor can envision a future with a congregation, he or she needs to know what changes to expect.

Spousal expectations. Many congregants are turned off by a highly visible, assertive pastoral partner, yet they are also disappointed if the spouse is a disengaged nonparticipant in the ministry. Between these extremes, a wide variety of involvement is possible. Seeking clarity on the congregation's view on the role to be played by your husband or wife is a requisite of the acquaintanceship stage.

Enrichment provisions. It is indeed true that *growing churches are pastored by growing ministers,* and staying fresh requires periods of stretching and recharging. While not appearing demanding, pastoral candidates must ascertain how the church feels about continuing education, participation at denominational meetings, personal involvements with mission trips, vacation time, and other Sundays out of the pulpit. Because no one can meet the needs of the future from past reserves alone, a church's plan for enrichment opportunities is important to know.

Salary range. Far too often, the first inkling a pastor has regarding compensation occurs during the final, official stage of candidating. The Bible commands churches to remunerate their shepherds generously and pastors to care for their family adequately, so it is remiss to accept an invitation to interview, let alone actively candidate, without knowing the salary range for the position. As was mentioned earlier, the precise salary—commensurate with experience and degree of responsibility—is best negotiated after the interview, but a ballpark figure for both salary and benefits should be discussed up front. A healthy relationship maintains openness, including forthrightness regarding compensation.

Pastoral track record. Just as a congregation will ask a prospective pastor to describe previous ministerial employment, so is the pastor free to ask about the church's relationships with previous ministers. Pastoral track records provide insight on how a congregation responds to and cares for its leaders. One pastor suggests asking a predecessor, "What kind of problems did you encounter? What did you seek to do and why? Why did you leave? What kind of pastor do you feel the church needs now and why?" And, "If I were to take this church, what three pieces of advice would you offer?"[1] Although unique factors affect every relationship, congregational past performance paints a picture of what a minister's relationship with the new church might look like.

References. By this time in their dating relationship, both minister and congregation will have exchanged a significant amount of data. *No surprises* has been their mutual goal. But, so far, both parties have presented only their own interpretation of themselves, which may be colored by what they have chosen to disclose. For this reason, congregations typically ask potential candidates for references, even asking those references to suggest other sources to check.

The practice of reference checking is equally wise for the clergy. One colleague suggests that a prospective pastor solicit information from "a neighbor near the church who does not attend, a near-by minister within the same denomination, and two individuals who left the church recently, one happy with the ministry and one unhappy."[2]

The acquaintanceship stage, during which prospective pastor and search committee become familiar with one another, can last many months. Usually, the process includes an initial contact, the sending of resume and/or questionnaire, an exchange of information (as outlined earlier), a visit by representative(s) of the search team, and a conference call with the whole committee and/or church governing board. If both parties believe the pastor/church union has strong possibilities, they will probably agree to enter the next stage in the relationship.

Going Steady: The Interviews

Going steady is a serious matter. Rarely is a ring given in pledge of marriage without careful thought by both parties. An invitation to interview with a church is just as serious. Too often, pastors agree to interview for the purpose of gaining more information, but scheduling an interview should occur only after a healthful exchange of information has left both parties still interested in pursuing the relationship.

The campus visit allows a prospective candidate and a search committee to meet and interact face to face. Issues raised in correspondence and telephone conversations may now be addressed on a more personal level. Full communication, including facial expression and body language, provides needed insight into one another's expectations.

Most ministers stress the importance of interviewing with one's husband or wife present. Unfortunately, churches concerned with expenses may want to invite the spouse only to the candidating event. This arrangement is unacceptable, for it places an inordinate amount of pressure on a marital partner. It is easier for a spouse to say, "Let's not pursue this further" after an interview than to come to that conclusion during the candidating weekend.

Frequently, the best appraisal of a potential ministry match comes from the cleric's partner. Failing to heed a spouse's negative vibes is foolish. One minister shared this illustration:

> During the two years we were at the church she never said 'I told you so!' but she might well have. It had happened almost as exactly as she feared. I should have known that my life partner ought to be the one who knew me best. I should have listened more intently to her caring instincts. She, of all people, knew my strengths and weaknesses, and felt from the beginning that this 'new marriage' might be a mismatch. Candidating pastors ought to appreciate their spouse's insights and not reject them lightly as I did. I firmly believe that when God calls, he calls both husband and wife, and there is something amiss if both partners are not hearing the same clear call.[3]

Since a successful ministry marriage begins with authenticity, during the interview both parties should be as transparent as possible. Overselling or underselling one's qualifications is detrimental. Forthright, precise answers are a must. Career counselors advise never to give an answer that is shorter than twenty seconds or longer than two minutes . . . nobody wants to listen to a monologue. People want succinct, quick answers.[4]

A good interview also includes a balance of interchange. Dick Bolles offers this advice:

> First, the candidate should talk half of the time about himself and half about the position. If candidates don't talk at all about themselves, people think they're chameleons who are willing to be whatever the parish wants them to be.

And nobody wants a chameleon. They want somebody whose behavior they can predict. The second half of the conversation is about the parish. The successful candidate wants to get the committee to talk. Research has discovered that people most likely to get hired stick to this fifty-fifty ratio talk about the candidate and the church.[5]

What types of questions do search committees ask? Denominational executives suggest that search committees ask the following questions:

1. What do you consider your spiritual gifts to be?
2. What aspects of pastoral ministry bring you greatest joy and fulfillment? What aspects of ministry are hardest for you? How do these relate to your strengths and weaknesses?
3. How do you assure a growing personal relationship with Christ? What guidelines have you found helpful in your personal walk with the Lord?
4. Could you tell us the approximate time schedule you would follow in a typical week of ministry at a church?
5. If you became our pastor, what special objectives would occupy you during your first six months?
6. What would people sense about you that would cause them to believe you loved them?
7. Do you consider your formal education complete? If not, what goals do you have for further formal training? Do you have aspirations to write a book?
8. How do you protect yourself from becoming overextended?
9. State your policy regarding officiating at weddings where divorce is involved.
10. What are your hobbies? Your favorite sports?
11. How does your family contribute to your life and ministry?
12. What is your present salary package?
13. Do you have a philosophy of ministry for the local church? If so, describe it.
14. How do you do the work of an evangelist?
15. How would you assist members of the church to improve their

evangelism ministry?

16. How would your pastoral leadership fulfill Jesus' command to make disciples? Are you comfortable in one-on-one situations designed to lead the other person to become a reproducing disciple?

17. How do you feel about small group ministries? What has been your personal involvement?

18. What is your personal practice regarding visitation?

19. How do you prepare the details of a worship service?

20. How do you feel about lay participation in reading, praying, sharing, giving announcements, etc.?

21. To what extent are the worship hours your evangelistic opportunity?

22. How much time do you invest in preparing a thirty-minute sermon?

23. What is your preaching style?

24. How much time do you need to deliver a sermon?

25. What do you envision your role in relation to a missions committee in developing the missionary work of the church?

26. How should a local church fund its missions program?

27. What is your feeling and evaluation of our denomination's missions program?

28. Would you desire to include parachurch groups in the mission work of the church?

29. What strategy do you follow for recruitment of volunteers?

30. How would you interface with the Sunday school, children's church, club programs, youth groups, and weekday preschool?

31. Do you consider yourself well organized? Illustrate.

32. How would you contribute to the skill-building of the leadership?

33. If you recommended employing a part-time secretary and the deacons thought that sufficient funds were not available for that purpose, how would you respond?

34. Have you a preference for the single-board structure? Would you feel comfortable under a multiple-board system?

35. What is the nature and scope of the pastor's authority in the

church? Please illustrate.

36. Do you have any outstanding financial obligations?
37. What strategies would you suggest for stimulating generosity of congregants?
38. What policies do you follow in personal counseling?
39. What is your premarital counseling requirement? [6]

Hopefully, not all of these questions would be asked at an interview—or little time would remain for the pastor to query the church. Whether a minister proceeds to candidating is, after all, a two-way decision. Therefore, the interview should also provide time for his or her follow-up on information received earlier through correspondence and conversations.

What types of questions should you—as a prospective candidate—ask a search committee? I suggest the following questions:

1. Why are you a member of this church? (Ask each of the members around the room to give a brief response.)
2. Why am I of particular interest to you?
3. What has been the most significant historical event in the life of the congregation? What has been the most notable in the last five years?
4. What are the highest priorities of your church? (Ask each participant to give three top priorities. Addressing priorities identifies not only important ministerial functions but also the amount of agreement among the committee members regarding those expectations.)
5. What was the most surprising fact you learned about the congregation from your self-study? (Again, a circle response will ensure feedback even from the less talkative members of the committee.)
6. Describe what an average week would look like for your next pastor.
7. Are there specific things that pastors should do that laypeople should not do?
8. If you were to rank the items in your doctoral statement and covenant, what would be your top two? (Again, encourage

multiple responses.)

9. What is the consensus level within your church regarding the issues of the role of women, divorced persons in leadership, charismatic gifts, and social issues? (Through earlier communications, a prospective pastor receives the official church policy. But now it is time to probe regarding depth of acceptance of the particular official position. Also inquire about other concerns that are still unresolved in the congregation.)

10. What activities engage the church with the local community? (Asking about immediate neighbors, policies about the use of facilities by outside groups, and local civic concerns reveals attention to maintenance versus outreach.)

11. Describe the typical attender at your church.

12. What is the biggest fiscal challenge at the church? If the church received a gift of $50,000, how would the congregants want to spend it?

13. What are the parameters for pastoral decision making? For example, who determines invitations to guest speakers, use of the church buildings by outsiders, or whom the pastor may marry?

14. What types of programs would you like to see started in the next two years? (After a circle response, ask appropriate follow-up questions, such as, *Why haven't they been started already? What might impede them from happening in the future?*)

15. If the congregation were to look in a mirror, what would it see as its strengths and weaknesses?

16. If you could change the church's facility, what would it look like? (During the tour of the campus, a potential candidate can observe repair of facilities, adequacy of heating and cooling systems, size of classrooms, quality of sound system, pleasantness of nursery [cleanliness and quality of toys and cribs], signage, decor of rest rooms, manicure of lawns, and functionality of office layout. Probing into how the facilities could be modified reveals how the congregation feels about its facilities.)

17. What would the ideal pastor's spouse at this church look like? With whom might he or she be compared?

18. How should your pastor(s) recharge their batteries? What means

of support does the church provide to encourage personal and professional enrichment?

19.   What has been the church's practice regarding pastoral salaries and benefits? On what basis have adjustments been made?

20.   What has been the procedure to determine the remuneration for this position? With whom will I meet during this visit to talk about the compensation package?

21.   Please tell me about the contributions of your last three pastors. What did they do particularly well? What legacy did they leave the church? What areas of greater expertise did they need?

When a couple is going steady, they deepen in mutual understanding and commitment. Sometimes this closeness reveals differences significant enough to merit breaking off the relationship. Most often, however, those who have reached this level of commitment proceed to the altar. Similarly, when pastor and call committee come through the interview process feeling excited about a possible union, it's time to plan a candidating event.

The Engagement Party: Candidating

The candidating experience, much like an engagement party, is a time of confirmation and celebration that usually includes the setting of a wedding date. The pastor being courted will greet scores of people, go through formalities, answer questions, and fellowship around food as a prelude to accepting the church's official proposal. For this reason, pastors should agree to candidate only when they are convinced that, barring some unforeseen circumstances, they would accept a call if it were extended.

The length of the candidating event varies from church to church. Some congregations use an eight-day schedule, allowing two Sundays for preaching and the whole week between for meeting people and exploring the community. Most churches, however, prefer to set aside one long weekend for the experience.

For several reasons, many colleagues recommend a Thursday-through-Monday schedule. First, a proper exchange of information during the previous months reduces the need for vast amounts of discovery. Second, it is fairly easy for pastor and spouse to absent themselves from their present church without raising suspicions. And third, congregational votes tend to be more a show of confidence in the search committee than a decision about the candidate. A typical member will affirm the recommendation of a highly trusted, credible search team but will have doubts about a candidate proposed by a controversial call committee. Unless a candidate self-destructs in their presence, most congregants are ready to affirm the search committee's recommendation after a weekend encounter.

If you have been invited to a candidating event, what should you expect? Getting the feel for the entire congregation, as well as letting them all become acquainted with who you really are, is your focused task for the weekend. While you should avoid putting on airs, you must remember that you will never get a second chance to make a first impression. One colleague asserts, "Upon first meeting you, therefore, they will be looking for those signs and symbols that indicate that you do like them—the way you shake hands, the way you listen to them, the kind of eye contact they have with you, the nonverbal signals you give that indicate your readiness and openness to engage them personally."[7]

Part of being yourself is presenting a candidating message typical of your usual performance. An appropriate message avoids controversial issues or peculiar viewpoints. Instead, it offers solid exposition applicable to a general audience. The sermon should not be unusually creative (i.e., dramatic first person or using PowerPoint, etc.) unless that is your normal practice. The most convincing message is a well-prepared sermon that is a realistic picture of your potential.

As you preach the candidating message, you should also look for information about the parishioners. How attentive is the audience? Are people using their Bibles? Are they taking notes? Do their facial expressions reveal interest? The congregation's involvement with your preaching gives much insight into their spiritual hunger.

The degree of congregational warmth is observable through the atmosphere present during social gatherings. Cues worth noting are the greetings of people, the expression on their faces, the enthusiasm of their singing, and their participation in conversations. The congregation's sense of self-esteem is discernable from the chemistry that exists between its members.

During your interview on campus, you had a chance to see the church's buildings. But now you can get a feel for the adequacy of the facilities. Observing the nursery in operation, the Sunday school class in progress, the traffic flow in the foyer, the capacity of the parking lot, and the attendance in the auditorium is more revealing than mere building diagrams and statistical records.

Sealing the Vows: The Letter of Call

After days of meetings, conversations, and impressions, the congregation (suitor) will vote (pop the question), and you must respond. A pastor who receives less than an 80 percent call may want to reconsider the potential for success with the new church. Better an embarrassing refusal than an ill-fated marriage! Fortunately, this occurrence is rare among those who have exercised wisdom before the candidating event.

On the other hand, a minister who is uncomfortable with less than a unanimous call might be asking too much. Since congregants rarely agree on every parish issue, a unanimous call may even be misleading. A positive call falls between the range of 80 to 100 percent and communicates a basic affirmation that the members are responsive to who you are as a person and will support the ministry into which you will lead them.

Protocol suggests that the chairman of the search committee notify you in person or by phone immediately after the voting results are tallied. Your response to this unofficial call is likewise unofficial. Formal acceptance is presented to the church in writing, following receipt of the church's official letter of call, which should state all of the specifics of the contractual arrangement (see fig. 6, "Sample Letter of Call," at the end of this chapter). If particulars are not spelled out, or if some of the specifics are different from your prior understanding, those differences should be resolved before sending a letter of acceptance. Follow-through on verbal agreements is difficult with volunteers rotating in and out of leadership, so it is advisable to document arrangements in writing.

A letter of acceptance should include (or verify) the anticipated starting date. Many pastors suggest forty-five to sixty days following the call as the best time to begin the new work. Your present congregation deserves at least thirty days' notice to handle the loss (especially if it is unexpected) and develop plans for the interim. Remaining longer than two months keeps both congregations on hold, draining energy and enthusiasm. A gracious good-bye promotes healthful closure for your people and releases them to pursue their work of transition (see chap. 15).

Summary

This year, Barbara and I celebrated our thirty-fifth wedding anniversary. I still remember that special day in September when *in the sight of God and company* we began our new life together. The longevity of our marriage not only speaks of God's goodness but also attests that years earlier we had begun a journey that drew us ever closer to each other.

Interestingly, this year also marks our thirty-fifth year of ministry. Over the years we've experienced new beginnings in Colorado, Arizona, New Jersey and Minnesota. None of our decisions to move was easy, but we made all of them with certainty. The fine ministry relationships we have experienced also speak of God's goodness and the careful courtship process that led us safely to each new destination.

Figure 6

Sample Letter of Call

Dear _____:

It is our privilege and joy as chairperson of the Pastoral Search Committee and Church Clerk to write this letter to report to you the positive action of the _____ Church to call you to become our senior pastor.

At the special business meeting held on _____ the church members expressed their appreciation of your ministry with us and voted to extend a call to you to become our pastor. The vote was as follows:

_____ Affirmative _____ Negative

We promise you our unified support, encouragement and positive obedience in the Lord. We promise and commit ourselves to the following compensation arrangements so you may fully devote yourself to lead us in ministry and outreach in our community.

1. Salary:
   $_____ per year. To be paid:
   $_____monthly; $_____biweekly; $_____weekly

2. Housing:
   Parsonage: _____; or,
   Housing allowance: _____
   Utilities: _____; or,
   Utility allowance: _____

3. Insurance:
   Medical: _____; Dental: _____; Retirement: _____
   Life: _____; Disability: _____; Other: _____

4. Business Expense:
    Car allowance: $_____
    Continuing education: $_____
    Books and periodicals: $_____
    Association meetings: $_____

5. Vacation:
    Annual: _____ weeks
    Special meetings: _____
    Study leaves: _____
    Days off per week: _____
    Sick leave/days per month: _____

6. Moving Expense: $_____

We further promise you our prayer support, acceptance of your leadership, and openness to the needs that may arise as you serve the Lord with us.

In anticipation of your positive response,

_____,

Chairperson

_____,

Church Clerk

Pastoral Search Committee of _____ Church[1]

---

1. Used by permission of Dr. Dennis Baker.

11

MOVING FROM ASSOCIATE TO SENIOR PASTOR

IF YOU ARE AN EFFECTIVE ASSOCIATE PASTOR, no doubt you've heard the words, "When are you going to get your own church?" No doubt, the members who posit these queries recognize your competence, for rarely is that comment made to an ineffective associate. In fact, one denominational executive notes, "You can decide you'd like to be a senior pastor, but if no one suggests it or no one asks you, that's an indicator that people don't see you in that role." So the affirming inquiry or compliment, especially when it is accompanied by an inner stirring toward a larger responsibility, may be pointing you to drive toward the senior pastorate.

Ministers traveling down the associate turnpike, however, should not change lanes too quickly. If leaving one ministry position for a similar one requires careful assessment, then sound counsel is even more important when one moves into a new ministry role altogether. Associates who are considering this possibility will benefit from interviewing ministers in that position and by asking specific questions of themselves.

Interview Senior Pastors

Congregations differ, senior pastors differ, and the health of their pastor/people relationships also differ. So obviously, asking colleagues about the pros and cons of the senior pastoral role will yield highly contextualized feedback. Nevertheless, when we consult with a variety of senior ministers, a clustering of responses will emerge.

You should feel free to ask as many questions as necessary to get a picture of the grass on the other side of the fence. However, as few as three general questions can still generate significant data. We do far better by limiting our questions and expanding our listening.

What do you like about your job? Just let these pastors talk. Listen to their tone as well as their words. About what are they enthusiastic? What energizes them? Ask clarifying questions, if necessary, but don't focus the questions so tightly that you lose the big picture of their highlights in the senior pastor role.

These colleagues can also fill you in on the lowlights from their perspective. So ask them, *What don't you like about your job?* If the word *job* sounds too secular, then feel free to refer to their calling, their role as senior minister, or their position as pastor. The bottom line is that you want their insights as to what's not that delightful on the side of the senior pastor fence.

As a final question, ask, *What are the weighty issues that you face as a senior minister?* A quick scan of the last six issues of *Leadership Journal* can reveal the types of things pastors wrestle with daily. But hearing directly from these colleagues what weighs heaviest upon them can help you decide whether you want to walk around in their shoes for the next ten years.

With their composite picture of the pastoral role now in mind, next ask yourself several questions regarding your fit in that role.

Ask Yourself Key Questions

Do I want to preach regularly? This might seem like a no-brainer. Obviously, if someone is considering a senior pastorate, he must want to preach more. But that's just the issue—how much more? Many associates presently preach once a quarter and some, perhaps, monthly. For many of them, the experience is invigorating. But weekly preparation and preaching is another story. In fact, some churches require more than one preaching preparation per week, plus occasional messages for funerals, weddings, and special occasions. One pastor reminds us, "The grind of sermon preparation never stops . . . the loop never closes."

One associate who made the move to a senior pastorate made this observation: "It didn't surprise me that I would have to work hard at preaching. But I underestimated the need for working out ahead, developing a year-long plan. It seems like now preaching is always on my mind." Another person who made the transition offered this interesting observation: "As an associate, I was always looking forward to an opportunity to preach. Now, as a senior, I always look forward to our missions conference, when I have a break from preaching." High-quality preaching is always a challenge. But if you increasingly find yourself studying the Scriptures, itching for opportunities to share your discoveries with the whole congregation, then you may enjoy the senior role.

Can I juggle many balls? The senior pastor of a large, multiple-staff church is, in reality, a specialist. But most ministers moving into their first senior pastorate will likely shepherd a small- to medium-size congregation. In these situations, the senior minister is involved in preaching, counseling, visitation, program oversight, and meetings. Add to this list additional situations that call for the pastor's attention: the vagrant seeking a handout, the missionary representative desiring visibility, the neighbor with a concern, and the denominational rep wanting assistance. And as one pastor reminds us, "People make it clear that they want to see the doctor, not the nurse."

Some people prefer to juggle a few balls really well; other people like to juggle many. Senior pastors do not have a choice. They are required to juggle several simultaneously, and it takes a certain gift mix both to enjoy the task and to do it well. So if you're like one colleague who shared, "I appreciated the variety . . . it was liberating compared to my old stratified job description," then perhaps you're ready for the transition into the senior pastor role.

Am I able to handle greater responsibility and stress? This question is closely related to the last one. It not only asks us to consider the number and diversity of activities that a pastor must manage but also highlights the increased weight of those responsibilities. One colleague commented, "I've had former associate staff members tell me that when they began their own senior pastoral ministries, they were amazed at the increased load and stress they now experienced." A second person remarked, "Associates considering a move to the senior pastorate need to understand the breadth and scope of the job . . . I had no comprehension of the pressure." And a third pastor voiced it thus: "When I was in the staff position my weekly schedule was fairly consistent and reasonable. But as a solo pastor, now I'm always on call."

The pressure that senior pastors sense comes from congregants who assume that a pastor should be outstanding in all areas of ministry. As one colleague shared, "You feel like the weight of the whole world is on your shoulders . . . the people feel like you should have expertise in every area." Another minister related the pressure of being on the inside thus: "Before I didn't have a clue on how much pain members of the congregation had in their lives—and now I know it all! The people in the church do not know the depth of these issues, nor can I share it with them, but the weight of knowing this stuff, and sometimes not knowing for sure how to respond, is heavy."

So the minister who thinks, *I don't need this ulcer*, might want to keep in the associate lane. However, the minister who says, "I can handle this—I'd love to see what I could do here," should consider the possibility.

Am I willing to take the flack that accompanies executive leadership? It's one thing to know the pressure of multiple responsibilities, but it's another thing to be the recipient of people's disgruntlement or pain. Pastors have been criticized over music styles, not marrying somebody's daughter, a problem in the youth group, an offended donor, and ministry directions, just to name a few issues.

Associates also receive their share of criticism. But the expression, *The buck stops at the top* is especially true for the senior pastor. Or, in the words of Don Meredith, "As you climb the flagpole higher, more people see your rear-end." Greater diversity of opinion exists on the role of the senior pastor than over the roles of the children's minister or counseling pastor.

Individuals with a thin hide, regardless of how much work they can handle, might not want to try the senior pastorate. However, if you understand that the point person draws the most fire yet believe that you can handle the flack, then perhaps you're ready for the transition into the role of the senior minister.

Am I more big-picture focused or more specifics focused? This question parallels the previous two questions. Some associates make their ministry area really sizzle, but they don't worry too much about the overall church program. Other associates continually see everything that needs attention, regardless of their ministry area. This might even get them into trouble simply because their inquiries cross boundary lines. Nevertheless, they simply cannot avoid the big picture. They instinctively think in light of the whole ministry, not just their area of service.

The issue here is connectivity and systemic thinking. One colleague who made the transition into the senior role described it thus: "I think the difference is between territorial thinking and global thinking." All ministers have to develop leadership, but an associate can develop leadership for the part, whereas the senior pastor has to develop leadership for the whole.

If you are wired to see the big picture, then you are probably ready for the generalist role. In fact, in the words of one pastor, "If you're chaffing under the leadership of your senior pastor, or if you need to work out your own dream, then you need to consider moving to a senior pastorate." Or as a district superintendent stated, "When you believe there are a larger number of things that you can do better than your senior pastor, and when that attitude becomes more frequent, you are probably feeling the nudge toward a senior pastorate."

If you find yourself always looking at the big picture, thinking holistically, then perhaps you're ripe for the transition to the senior minister role.

Advice for New Senior Pastors

Clarify expectations. Since the duties and responsibilities of senior pastors vary greatly, it is wise to establish expectations early in your ministry. Issues of boundaries should initially be discussed with the search committee. Most churches provide a position description in the candidate packet. Although search committees can easily delineate role functions, most have not taken time to prioritize those functions or to give a weekly allotment of time required for their execution. Honest discussions up front about your workload and giftedness can save some misunderstandings later.

Once you arrive at the church, and through your first years, continue to clarify expectations with the leadership. For example, one pastor who was not gifted in counseling agreed with the board that he would only do intake sessions with people in need. The board wanted his attention focused on the church's discipleship infrastructure, leaving counseling to the associate pastor and professionals who could best help those in need.

At the broader level, continue to clarify expectations with the congregation. In a positive way, let your people view the world of ministry. They need help seeing all of the opportunities before the congregation and where your calling and giftedness fit into the picture. An emphasis on ministry teams and the fact that every member is a minister spreads the responsibility for ministry across the congregation. One pastor shared, "I use the pulpit to let the congregation see ways in which I serve." Another colleague said that from the beginning of his ministry, he let the congregation know when he was available and when he was not: "I set my schedule early. I was very intentional on what got into my Franklin Planner. My secretary screens calls in the morning and allows a freer flow in the afternoon."

Being up front about your ministry schedule, and then communicating it regularly, helps you minimize unrealistic, and often competing, expectations.

Know the freedom of scheduling. Just as expenses push to exceed income, work expands to exceed available time. For this reason, it's important to work intentionally rather than reactively. Some colleagues schedule their activities in fifteen-minute increments. Others resist using a schedule altogether. Perhaps avoiding either extreme (being either driven or undisciplined) is the healthier balance. The big parts of your ministry—studying, planning, vision casting at lunch meetings, etc.—must take the biggest part of your schedule. By writing these events into your weekly calendars, you can reserve the time necessary for doing a quality job.

One of the biggest priorities for clergy is their families. Therefore, place family events, meals, and activities in your calendar first. To guard family time, one bold pastor responded to a parishioner seeking counsel by saying, "I'm sorry, but I need to be at my daughter's soccer game this evening." Most colleagues, however, give a more generic reply: "I'm sorry, I have an appointment this evening, but I could meet with you tomorrow at 2:00 P.M." Another pastor guards the family time with this practice: "When my kids were in the elementary years, I didn't take work home from the office. They were my evening schedule; in essence, they were my hobby. If they didn't need me on a given night, I had bonus time. I found this was better than resenting them when they wanted my attention, simply because I had scheduled in some studying or reading that evening."

The bottom line is that only you can take charge of your schedule. Letting others fill it up, or overprogramming it yourself, will squeeze out more important opportunities.

Prepare sermons early. One colleague has shared that his secret to effective preaching is *preparation, preparation, preparation!* More church members see their pastor on Sunday than see him in personal weekday contacts. In fact, in larger churches most people only *connect* with the pastor via the pulpit. Therefore, solid preparation and familiarity with the text are essential to maximize your primary presence with your people.

Early preparation begins with the preaching schedule. Many colleagues use an annual preaching calendar. Some plan from fall to fall, others from January to January. Some prefer to go textually through a book in the Bible; others prefer topics; still others follow a lectionary. The sooner you can determine your preaching direction, the easier it is to build the sermonic portfolio per message and to coordinate worship themes with textual selections.

Annual planning does not mean inflexibility, however. During a study leave in July, for example, a pastor may plan a five-part miniseries only to realize later that six Sundays will be needed to present the material properly. Sermons can be shortened, combined, lengthened, or presented in two parts. Your thorough weekly preparation will determine the final product. But using a long-term, directional plan will free you from wasted start-up time each week.

Regarding weekly preparation, many colleagues have found that a lot of preparation at the end of a week is not as good as heavier preparation at the beginning of a week. Here is one pastor's discovery: "When I finish the bulk of my sermon preparation by Wednesday, I am able to let it perk for the rest of the week. Then, as I review the sermon later in the week, a new idea or better way to say something may come to me. When I prepare late in the week, I forfeit this opportunity for review."

Delivery aids taken into the pulpit vary among preachers. Some pastors use a manuscript with key thoughts underlined. Others use only an outline. Some use a color code to attract their eye to main points [black], Scripture [red], or illustrations [blue]. A couple of my friends even just preach from a Bible with Post-It Notes surrounding the passage. Whatever format you develop, early preparation will raise your confidence in the pulpit.

Delegate effectively. The needs around us are so great, and the work of the ministry is so important, that no one person can handle it all. That is why God has given a complementary array of gifts to believers (1 Cor. 12), so that all can share in His "ministry of reconciliation" (2 Cor. 5:18). Effective pastoral ministry requires that the focus of your service always be the "equipping of the saints for the work of service" (Eph. 4: 12 NASB). For clergy survival and for each congregant's fulfillment, you must delegate ministry to those who are best equipped. A critical mark of your leadership effectiveness will be your ability to enlist and develop people for ministry.

Be careful how you delegate, however. Some people might misinterpret your passing off work to others as laziness. If it looks as though you are simply unloading ministry on others, you'll be in trouble.

When associate pastors are surveyed regarding their role as second fiddle, many of them agree with the observation of this colleague: "I don't mind playing second fiddle if first fiddle is competent and working hard. But it's tough to fiddle hard in a support role when the senior pastor seems to be coasting."

Effective delegation means becoming a student of your people and providing others with opportunities according to their calling and giftedness. As one pastor warns, "Empowering the right people to do the right job brings success to ministry. However, if you empower the wrong people, we're stuck, and ministry suffers!"

Your role as senior minister is one of *player-coach*. Yes, you have specific responsibilities in the game of congregational ministry, but your overall effectiveness will be measured to a large degree by how well the whole team performs. Again, the real issue is not so much how you shine in your responsibilities as it is how well the congregation shines in their service.

In your role as team builder, help your leaders understand the tasks and abilities of one another. Several churches, for example, have used a personality or leadership profile with their board to enable the members to develop an appreciation of one another. More specifically, one elder board used Inscape's *Innovate with C.A.R.E. Profile*[1] to discover who were the *Creators,* the *Advancers,* the *Refiners,* and the *Executors.* Just knowing that some people were wired to initiate new ideas whereas others were wired to assess them critically was very helpful. The process also helped them realize that the pastor, like each of them, had only one orientation/style; therefore, the whole team needed to move together for ministry effectiveness.

Have a dignified demeanor. The specifics of what is considered proper decorum for clergy varies from one congregation to another. Regarding dress, for example, in one church where I preach, I'm expected to wear a sport coat in the blended services and a sport shirt in the contemporary service. However, in another church in town, I'm required to wear a suit for each service, and it *must be buttoned when on the platform.* One pastor colleague summarized it thus: "While jeans and sneakers may work with the youth group, slacks and shoes are more appropriate when working cross-generationally."

Written communication should be clear and concise. Bulletin notes and newsletter articles can reveal our vision and passion. What might be appropriate for a youth column might need a more inclusive style when addressing the entire flock.

Dignified demeanor also means articulate oral communication. Words paint pictures, and those pictures should communicate effectively across the diversity within the congregation. A joke permitted in a youth group might be offensive from the pulpit. The clarity of your speech, the use of humor, the use of slang, and your dress should be at an appropriate level, or one level above the average member of the congregation.

Integrity means acknowledging source material when used. Authenticity also means opening your heart through personal stories and examples. A good balance is to avoid being overly detached from the content yet at the same time not overkilling personal and family illustrations.

Cast a vision. The kind of church you will pastor will be determined largely by the vision you cast among your people. In smaller congregations, history, tradition, and key families frequently govern ministry direction. As a congregation gets larger, it typically looks to representative leadership and, later, even more to the pastoral staff. Whatever the size or setting, the pastor has to assume leadership for mission and vision.

One colleague shares his vision thus: "I sell my dream of what kind of church we will be every time I meet with one of our leaders. It may be at a monthly board meeting, it may be during visitation, it may be at a lunch meeting—wherever it is, I always present what we can become in Christ." I like this pastor's strategy. It is fruitless to drop one vision load in a *state of the church* address and then complain that no one buys into it. Communicating that lost people matter to God, that we are to grow in our knowledge of Christ, and that we are born to serve requires a holistic strategy to infect the whole congregation.

Implement timely change. Many good books have been written on the subject of change, so there's no point in recounting that wealth of literature here. However, two issues are worth highlighting at this time.

First, we should remember *how* the change cycle works. It is not a mystery that people move through a predictable process regarding the adoption of an innovation. Knowing where they are in that process will allow you to help them move forward. Although people's resistance should not inhibit church leaders from proceeding with important changes, several practices can encourage receptivity to an innovation. Pastors can help their congregation by:

- Creating an atmosphere where change is acceptable
- Building trust in leadership
- Making sure a specific change is the best alternative
- Communicating change early and thoroughly
- Implementing change carefully
- Keeping all lines of communication open during implementation

The second issue concerns *when* to initiate change. Advisors typically suggest spending the first year at a new church just getting to know your people and letting them know your heart. Although this guideline is generally wise, your role as a change agent will vary contextually. In a smaller congregation, change must move slower. In larger congregations, especially those that have plateaued or are in decline, the new pastor is expected to make some early correctional initiatives.

Any congregation can change. The issue is really how much time is required and how much care is needed in the change process. Both a ski boat and an aircraft carrier can turn 180 degrees; the difference is how much water they need for the maneuver. Implementation of careful change is an art that can be mastered. It is an essential skill for effective ministry in any congregation.

Establish a peer support group. No doubt, by now you have already experienced the value of ministry colleagues. Some of us were blessed with excellent role models. Many of us have also known the blessings of colleague support. Although you will work closely with the leadership in your congregation, and perhaps even more closely with a couple of key leaders, the weight of the pastoral role and the complexity of ministry requires the sympathetic support and insights gained from other professionals.

These colleagues may be neighboring pastors or ministerial friends you've known for years. With some of them, you may meet monthly; with others, you may only keep in touch via the Internet. Whatever your practice, the collective wisdom and support available from colleagues in ministry is too important to ignore.

Unfortunately, because of the press of each week's calendar, you might be tempted to wait for your colleagues to set up the meeting. Don't do it; you take the initiative to schedule these valuable times together. For the sake of your safety, sanity, and success in ministry, ensure that colleague fellowship is prioritized into your monthly schedule.

Summary

Well, how do you feel after reading this chapter? Are you somewhat intimidated or rather energized? Are you thinking, *I've got it pretty good now; I'm not sure I want to jump into that scenario?* Or are you already dreaming of possibilities and ways your giftedness can fit into the scenario?

If you are seriously considering the senior pastor role and believe that you have the administrative gifts and preaching ability to lead the congregation effectively, then I suggest that you change lanes and drive toward the senior pastorate. Don't make the shift too quickly. Definitely be selective into which town you drive. But do move in this direction when external confirmation and opportunity converge with your internal passion and giftedness.

12

MOVING FROM SENIOR
TO ASSOCIATE PASTOR

A GENERATION AGO, CAREER-PATH MOVEMENT for clergy usually went from an assistant role to that of senior pastor. Today, however, a number of factors have changed that pattern. First is the growth of multiple-staff congregations. Hundreds of churches now minister to two thousand or more congregates each week. For each senior minister hired, dozens of staff specialists are employed. A seminary graduate or pastor now looking for a change in ministry will find more openings in associate roles than in senior pastorates.

Second, with the shrinking of rural America and the regionalization of services, fewer solo pastorates are available each year. Just as mom-and-pop stores are being replaced by nationwide chains, more than thirty-five hundred Protestant churches close their doors each year, with many members moving to full-service regional churches. Many church plants now even begin with a multiple staff, frequently utilizing part time personnel until they become larger.

Third, the high bar of expectations for senior ministers is being raised increasingly. Successful pastors today need to be excellent leaders and dynamic communicators. The changing culture around us has shrunk dramatically the need for institutional chaplains. Pastors today frequently find themselves playing the role of ethnographers, systems analysts, and futurists.

Fourth, many churches are now looking for a senior pastor who can reach the next generation of leadership within the church. *Builders* are rarely sought, and *Boomers* are becoming less attractive. But *thirty somethings* are in high demand. Frequently, churches look for someone under forty-five years of age who understands the postmodern culture. Therefore, tenured senior ministers will find less opportunity for senior pastorates, especially in larger churches, toward the end of their careers.

Fifth, many churches are no longer afraid to call an associate from a dynamic ministry to serve as their senior pastor. The standard practice was, "Let's find someone with senior pastoral experience." But too many churches have found that pulpit time in a smaller congregation is not as valuable as leadership experience in a larger, dynamic congregation. To lead a multiple-staff church, search committees are looking for someone who has been a part of a multiple-staff church. Therefore, many pastors of smaller congregations are passed over.

The route from associate to senior minister is no longer an expectation for many clergy. In fact, many colleagues now see themselves as intentional career associates. And many senior pastors are looking with new interest at the benefits of playing on a staff team.

Advantages of the Associate Pastorate

Colleagues who have changed lanes from the senior to the associate pastorate agree on a number of benefits of the associate role.

Ministry focus. Everybody wants a piece of the senior pastor, especially in smaller churches. The missionary wants an opportunity to speak, the mother requests a wedding for her pregnant daughter, and the betrayed spouse wants counsel. Everyone has expectations for the senior pastor, including the denominational executive, the shut-in, a local official, and the parents of a rebellious teenager. One pastor expressed it thus: "I left the senior pastorate because I wanted to specialize more in mentoring. The senior pastor's role has escalated in administration, so I moved to an associate in discipleship. This was a better fit for my life mission." While workloads of associates may be just as demanding, they are frequently more focused and, therefore, more manageable.

Higher quality in performance. The senior pastor's time is divided among so many areas that often he or she is performing well enough to survive but rarely to a level of excellence that is satisfying. Associate pastors, on the other hand, give 100 percent of their time to specialized areas; therefore, they can be more knowledgeable and competent in their particular field. Their level of job satisfaction is usually high because they don't have to excel across many areas. In the words of one colleague, "A senior pastor will disappoint a lot of people because you can't do everything well, and you can't be omnipresent."

Less pressure. Expectations are not as great for an associate. As an associate pastor, no one got on my case if elderly Mr. Smith could not hear the sermon. If the budget was behind, no one asked me to preach on tithing. If the visiting musical group was too upbeat, no one spoke to me after the service. But as a senior pastor, when the young people returned from a social at 3:00 A.M., I was called. And when the building program was launched, I was expected to motivate the funding.

One pastor related, "I found the associate pastorate to be a safer place—you don't get all the credit, but neither do you get all the blame." Likewise, another pastor asserted, "Senior pastors live with the fear of the pressure that they should have visited someone or helped someone and did not, and later they lived to hear about it." While associate pastors are held accountable for their area of ministry, the overall weight of congregational health does not rest upon them.

More congregational tolerance. Again, personally speaking, as an associate, my dress could be less formal, my grammar less precise, my candid observations less filtered, and my mistakes less critical. As a senior pastor, however, I needed to maintain the type of decorum discussed in the previous chapter. The situation is similar to politics: we are embarrassed when one of our diplomats commits a faux pas, but we are really troubled when the President makes an obvious blunder.

Deeper relationships. Thankfully, the era when pastors were advised not to make friendships in the congregation is over. Obviously, this is still a delicate area that can cause division in a church. However, because of the programmatic oversight of the associate's role, they are more likely to draw into both ministry and their lives people with similar passions and values.

For all of these reasons, many people considering a ministry transition are choosing to serve in a specialized field.

Role-Change Questions

Senior pastors considering the possibility of serving in an associate capacity should ask themselves several questions, including the following.

Do I have a good understanding of the particular specialization I am considering? Although an answer to this question may be found in books on multiple-staff ministry or by studying position descriptions, the best source of fresh information comes from colleagues serving in that particular field. Ask them questions about the pros and cons of the role as well as the gift mix and competencies required to perform it effectively. Listen to both their tone and their words. What energizes them and excites them? What challenges and frustrates them? What is their relationship with the senior pastor? Obviously, each respondent will be sharing from his or her own perspective. Nevertheless, after several interviews, common themes should surface that will help you assess your interest and fit for this role.

Am I a generalist or a specialist? Some people are wired to take charge. They are comfortable being in control. They are not necessarily so much controlling as a big-picture person. Such individuals are bothered by glitches in the sound system, the appearance of the shrubbery on the church property, the quality of the newsletter, and the overcrowded parking lot. Although these issues are not part of their job description, they are still vexed in spirit and push for qualitative improvement.

If you can identify with this type of desire to influence everything, then you should probably remain in a senior pastor role, or perhaps you could serve as an executive pastor or church administrator. Big-picture people working as associates can get resentful over things beyond their control. However, if you can *brighten the corner where you are*, then an associate staff position may be a good match.

For what ministry specialization am I equipped and about which do I have passion? Some larger churches employ a senior associate to perform general pastoral functions. But most churches rarely look for generic associates. Therefore, as a generalist considering a move to a staff position, think about what specifics within your pastoral ministry bring you greatest fulfillment. Do you enjoy socializing with seekers, and does presenting Christ to them energize you? Do you find yourself deeply invested in the small-group movement in your church, possibly leading a couple of groups yourself? Or do you believe the annual missions conference is the high point of the year, always looking for opportunities to involve people in short-term projects? Identifying your specific passions and expertise will help you narrow your job search and find a fitting role.

How badly will I miss preaching? Most churches have only Sunday morning preaching opportunities; therefore, associates typically have very little time in the pulpit. For some, such as this colleague, the change was welcomed: "While I miss regular preaching opportunities, I had to admit to myself that I just wasn't the greatest preacher. I love studying the Scriptures and crafting a message, but I am just not that captivating in the pulpit." Other pastors have shared similar relief after they weren't part of the *sermon grind* anymore. Interestingly, many associates have found that they now teach more people in their large Sunday school class than they did previously in their smaller church, and each quarter they have the freedom either to teach or to invite another person to lead the class.

Most such pastors admit that it was hard at first to sit in the auditorium and listen to another preacher, especially without analyzing the senior pastor's hermeneutical interpretation, content, and delivery. However, many of us eventually have come to a point where we can hear from the Lord through the preparation and delivery of an appreciated colleague.

If you think that you can make that transition without feeling resentful over the loss of pulpit exposure, then you can serve successfully as an associate.

Can I enjoy playing second fiddle? In our heads, we know that second fiddles play an essential part. We honestly believe that the harmony offered makes the music sweeter. But some pastors who make the transition admit that it's difficult to keep their eyes on the conductor; instead, they keep coveting the position of first chair. One associate advises, "When you go from first fiddle to second fiddle, you have to understand clearly who you are and what you are called to do, or else when the accolades go to the first fiddle, that can be a real point of contention and frustration."

When I was in seminary, a well-know associate minister offered this advice: "If it bothers you that the senior pastor gets a turkey at Thanksgiving, or is offered a week in some plush condo, and you are not, then just become a senior pastor. The bottom line is those perks might not be handed out to associates."

Some senior ministers, unhappy with this reality, try to challenge such favoritism; some of them are the greatest cheerleaders of their staff. However, others are oblivious to the perceived inequities. Some even display a sense of entitlement to these perks. Regardless of the attitude of the first fiddle, however, if you believe that you could enjoy playing a good harmony part, then you could probably make the transition to the associate role.

Advice for New Associate Pastors

Accelerate your learning curve. Although a few associate staff members will find positions as preaching associates, most will assume the role of a specialist. Those with administrative gifts may be called to an executive pastor position. Others may move into pastoral care. Some of our colleagues have become pastors of discipleship, ministers of assimilation, directors of outreach, directors of development, pastors of community life, and ministers to senior adults, to name a few of these specialized roles. Each of these jobs requires a particular knowledge base and skill set for effective ministry. In some of these fields, a great body of literature exists, such as in the specialization of small groups. Other fields, such as in the area of adult communities, have fewer resources available. Most, however, have conferences that focus on the various needs of these types of specialized ministries. In addition, tenured colleagues who have served successfully in these positions will gladly share their insights.

As a senior pastor, you may have heard of the *Alpha* program, but if you become a minister of outreach, you will need to know the pros and cons of this program. Likewise, as a senior minister you may have used some of the Willow Creek/Zondervan small group resources, but as a discipleship pastor, you'll need to know that product line, as well as materials from Navigators, InterVarsity Press, Lifeways, and so forth, to determine what's best for your congregation.

As specialists, associates are expected to be experts in their concentration. Although people may appreciate your general pastoral presence, ultimately they will evaluate you on the contribution you make in the specific area for which you were hired.

Serve missionally. Most churches cannot afford enough professional staff to lead the full-service ministry they desire. For this reason, much of a pastor's time is absorbed by program administration. Frequently, a pastor inherits a program, so it is easy to get consumed with program planning, staffing, and execution without asking the bigger questions of purpose and mission.

Associate staff over specific programs need to ask how their particular ministry fulfills the church's overall vision. In addition, each particular department would benefit by specifying their own purpose statement. Then strategic initiatives can be planned each year and executed to accomplish the mission.

Too often in a new setting, we're tempted just to jump in and start doing ministry. But for the best kingdom impact, even within our specific ministry niche, we should ensure that we are not only doing things right but also doing the right things.

Bless the senior pastor. As one who has *lived there*, no one else in the congregation knows better the difficulty of the senior pastoral challenge; therefore, as associates, we "should look not only to [our] own interests, but also to the interests of others" (Phil. 2:4), especially those of the senior pastor. We can sincerely pray for and work toward God's best for their ministry. We can offer the blessings of respect, intercession, and praise. We can become a sounding board, encourager, and confidant if so entrusted. We can keep the senior pastor in the loop with information that will help him shepherd the flock. In addition, if asked, we can accept responsibilities that go beyond our job description.

Let's be careful of our own expectations, however. We are also the most likely among the associate staff to think that we know what is best in a given situation. Because we have called many of the shots before, we may even think that we deserve greater receptivity of our suggestions. Let's avoid the pitfall of being a colleague who always grouses that "they never ask for my opinion." Instead, let's offer an observation when it's requested but meanwhile support the directions of the leader selected by the congregation.

Develop good working relationships with other associate staff. Healthy churches rarely have prima donna individualists running departments. Most often, they are staffed by a team of gifted yet humble leaders. The synergy of their work together maximizes their efforts. They love the Lord, respect one another, serve passionately, and enjoy the people to whom they minister.

Developing a good relationship with other members of the pastoral staff does not mean that we automatically become friends with everybody. Just as in all of life, you are naturally drawn to some people and not others, so too, as a staff member, different levels of friendship will develop. A good working relationship means that we develop a genuine concern for our colleagues and their areas of service.

A loving camaraderie means that we are patient and kind. We are not envious, boastful, or proud. We are not rude to one another or self-seeking. We are not easily angered and do not keep records of wrong. We try to protect our colleagues, always trust them, and always work for their well-being (paraphrase of 1 Cor. 13:4–7).

Understanding the *passion* and *personal styles* of the other members of the staff will help you work in better harmony. Listening to their stories will tell you much. For example, a driven, doer-type colleague wants to know *the what* of an issue whereas the conscientious, calculating colleague wants to know *the how* of a situation. An ideal way for the professional staff to gain insight into one another is to work with a ministry coach who can administer assessment profiles useful for team building. A church really gets humming when the entire leadership team is working effectively.

Avoid triangulation. It is not uncommon for a member of the congregation to approach a pastor to talk or even vent about a church situation. Frequently, underlying the criticism are misunderstandings or just personal preferences. Sometimes the criticism moves past a program to the colleague responsible for the program.

While we want to be polite, empathetic listeners, we can never allow the demeaning of a colleague. Triangulation at any level must be avoided; therefore, redirecting the person to the party concerned is our wisest course of action.

Develop ministry teams. As was stated before, a church cannot afford to pay enough people to run all of the ministries it desires. Even if it could hire a visitation pastor to do all of the visiting, for example, that practice would violate the pastoral charge of Ephesians 4:11–12 to develop others to carry out that work. Since no one has all of the time and giftedness necessary for effective ministry, your ministry success will depend on the multiple teams you put together to accomplish your missional objectives.

Ministry teams differ from committees in that each member is a player. Thankfully, the ineffective structure of people making decisions for others to implement is disappearing in many churches. It is being replaced by the more effective approach of ministry teams responsible for assessment, decision making, and ministry operations.

People today are becoming less interested in filling someone else's ministry slot. They want to serve from their own passion and giftedness. And although many people are tired of doing church jobs, those same people get excited about the ownership of lay pastoring. Therefore, good scouting, recruiting, training, and empowering of solid ministry teams maximize your service.

Practice the three V's. Frequently, I tell associate staff members to remember three words that begin with the letter *V.* I encourage them first to *be valuable.* The best way for an associate pastor to help a senior pastor is to do his or her task well. The church will benefit from and the senior pastor will appreciate an associate who maintains a good attitude, is loyal, and is happy to serve in his or her assigned area. However, the most valuable staff members not only cover their own base but also are willing to help when there is a need in another area of ministry. Helping out with a visit, a task force assignment, or a funeral makes this type of team player valuable.

Second, *be visible*. The influence of an associate is directly related to his or her visibility and involvement in the life of the overall church. If you have comfortable platform presence, then accept opportunities to make announcements or offer the morning prayer. If your schedule allows you to attend various congregational socials, then jump at these chances to know your people better. Many of our colleagues have acknowledged that it's in these "fishing pool" settings that they've become familiar with people who down the road became significant leaders in their ministries.

Third, *be vulnerable*. As associates, we can share our concerns with the senior pastor without dumping on him or pressuring him to meet specific needs. We can be honest about our strengths as well as those areas in which we just don't shine. When the time comes for annual review, accept the pastor's appraisal. Even if you think that the evaluation is not accurate, it still provides an understanding of how your supervisor perceives your ministry. Since his perceptions are reality to him, you need to know those feelings. No one I know really enjoys doing staff evaluations. An honest openness on your part makes it easier for the pastor to help you with focused feedback.

Meet regularly with a colleague support group. In the previous chapter, I advised senior pastors to get involved in a colleague support group. Likewise, for both your professional development and personal encouragement, seek to meet regularly with other ministers. Ideally, this peer group would be composed of colleagues in a similar role context and congregation size. Preferably, these resource confidants are not from your own pastoral staff or among the lay people within the congregation. Although you may have friendships from your own setting, a ministry accountability group is most beneficial when it is more neutral.

Some of our colleagues meet regularly with their peer groups whereas others just get together occasionally to bring each other up to speed on their ministries, share prayer requests, and discuss ministry insights. Some of them use an intentional curriculum, studying together a resource or personal growth book. One group that I know gets away twice a year for a two-day retreat together. Another group goes out of state for a few days to meet with a resource mentor. The specifics of group practice will evolve over time.

For now, as you move into a new ministry context, set aside at least one lunch meeting a week to begin to know ministry colleagues in other churches, then see which relationships begin to click. Soon, some of these relationships will develop into encouraging friendships.

Summary

A number of years ago, a large congregation was looking to fill two associate positions. The two individuals whom they finally called had both served before as senior pastors. Another congregation currently has three former senior pastors serving as associates on their staff. What both of these churches have found is that these associates bring a new level of maturity, understanding, and team spirit to their congregation. They understand the demands on their senior minister and stand loyally behind him.

These colleagues also enjoy a new freedom that they have found as associates. No one in their congregations ask them, "When are you going to get your church?" They recognize that these competent former senior pastors have selected their current role based on personal gifting, self-awareness, and ministry call. Their churches are healthy and growing, not just because of a competent senior minister but because of their excellent pastoral team.

If you've been driving down the senior pastor turnpike and think the highway described in this chapter might be a better route for you, then weigh carefully this transition, and see what new direction the Lord may open up for you.

13

MOVING FROM CONGREGATION TO MARKETPLACE

NEARLY EVERYONE WHO ENTERS PROFESSIONAL Christian service assumes that they're embarking on a long-term career. They hear the stories about those who have *left the ministry,* but they can't imagine that it might happen to them. Most ministers just jumped into the pastorate, assuming that any changes in service would be one of setting but not career.

In reality, however, unwanted transitions are a growing problem in churches. A national study of U.S. pastors revealed that

- Nine out of ten pastors (91 percent) know three to four others who have been forced out of pastoral positions.
- One-third of all pastors (34 percent) serve congregations who either fired the previous minister or actively forced his or her resignation.
- Ten percent of dismissed predecessors left pastoral ministry.
- Nearly one-fourth (23 percent) of all current pastors have been forced out at some point in their ministry.
- In their most recent experience, 13 percent were fired directly, 58 percent were forced to resign, and the remaining 29 percent resigned because of perceived, but not overt, pressure.[1]

When ministry settings close to pastors, most of them are able to find another place of church service, but a significant number of ministers are choosing to leave vocational ministry each year. Some of them make the transition because of burnout, others because of perceived failure, and still others because of moral indiscretion. While focused counsel is beneficial in each recovery process, a general transition strategy can guide pastors who are embarking on this major career change.

A Theology of Call

How people feel about leaving vocational service is directly related to how they first felt about their call to ministry. In chapter 2, we noted that both classical and contemporary writers articulate at great length their side of the sovereign direction/personal choice perspectives regarding call to ministry, yet they are less dogmatic on whether this is a life-long call.

In that initial chapter, we concluded that pastoral ministry typically follows a convergence of compulsion, character, competencies, and confirmation. It is logical, therefore, that an erosion or disappearance of any of these factors will likewise lead a pastor away from career service.

Some colleagues who have moved from church to marketplace saw their *compulsion* change. One pastor confessed, "Ministry was like pushing a rope; I just didn't want to do that any more." Another responded, "I began to get more excited about working as a business minister more than a professional minister." Christian ministry is too consuming to attempt it half-heartedly. A move to another type of work is in order if the compulsion is gone.

Some pastors have left church service because of *character* issues. The most notable and immediate grounds for termination are sexual indiscretion or financial impropriety. The issue is one of trust. If members of the flock cannot trust their shepherd, he or she cannot lead. While those two acts usually result in immediate termination, other character problems can also push a minister out of church service. Insensitivity, arrogance, argumentativeness, sarcasm, and a preoccupation with personal agenda are all credibility busters and can push the offender away from vocational service.

The *competency* factor that draws one into ministry can also lead a person out of career service. One pastor described the experience that many colleagues are facing today: "Someone changed the rules in the game. In seminary, I was trained to be a shepherd, and this role worked well in my early years in the church. But now congregations want a CEO/visionary leader/manager, and that's a different skill set." Some colleagues who have experienced such cultural changes have successfully switched roles within the church. But others have chosen to use their competencies in careers outside of the church.

A movement away from vocational service is also required when *confirmation* is removed. A pastor may want to keep leading, but if the flock quits following or leaves for other pastures, his ministry there is over.

Sometimes the withdrawal of confirmation is sudden. One shocked pastor explained, "I opened my eyes after the morning benediction and saw that the deacon board had come to the platform. They called for a special business meeting and voted me out that morning." Fortunately, most churches are not that cruel. The withdrawal of confirmation, if it happens, is usually more gradual. One colleague related, "Though I had survived several votes of confidence, I knew the church was languishing, and I felt the leadership needed to go on without me." Regardless of how the congregation may express their discontent, if they no longer desire your service, a change is needed.

The pain or guilt associated with moving from remunerated ministry varies greatly among those who have made the transition. And although time gives perspective and supposedly *heals all wounds*, some colleagues still feel the pain even years later. The more deeply they perceived the victimization, the longer the recovery. And the more they felt that they had disappointed others (spouse, parents, mentor, or congregates), the longer their guilt remained. Conversely, the more control the individuals had in the decision, the more fully they healed and the more quickly they became excited about new directions.

In the crucible of this transition, many colleagues have expressed that it's hard to see the light at the end of the tunnel. But those who have successfully navigated the change are quick to remind us that they are still in ministry. They enjoy the kingdom impact they are making in the marketplace and welcome the less-pressured volunteer role they now play in the church.

Travelers through this transition have discovered that although a particular congregation might be finished with their service, God is never finished with their service. This is the conviction of one colleague who, when asked, "Are you hoping to get back into ministry?" responded, "I *am* in ministry!" Another pastor affirmed, "God still wants to use you." Another shared, "There is still plenty of ministry in the field. Right now, for example, a fellow employee who is in an affair and doesn't know what to do has asked me for counsel." And another joyfully related, "I have talked with more lost people about Christ this past year than I did in both pastorates. I am really charged by the opportunity that this job has given me to talk to people about Christ."

There is ministry beyond the church. In fact, many former pastors have found marketplace ministry to be a liberating, joyful, and effective place of harvest. The successful movement into this new realm begins with a solid understanding of the phases of transition.

Understanding Transition

Every transition is similar, yet every transition is unique. Each moves through common phases, however, each is deeply personal. Three analogies can provide understanding for people who are making the transition from congregation to marketplace: the stages of grief related to dying, the Exodus of Israel, and the aerial trapeze.

The stages of grief associated with death and dying may also be experienced by others going through loss.[2] People grieve losses that are physical, emotional, and even vocational. The predicted phases of grief flow from denial to anger, to bargaining, to depression, and finally to acceptance.

A pastor's initial response to a closing ministry door is *denial*. Denial surfaces in many forms. A minister may think that she is being judged unfairly, or that her critics are only few. Or he may think that if he just works harder things will get better. One pastor shared, "I thought if I could just stay one year longer, I'd win their hearts." Another colleague described it thus: "I had always heard that it's only about ten people who force most pastors out of their church. At that time, I didn't believe that an even larger group felt my ministry was over." And another colleague admitted, "I knew people were leaving the church, but I justified it as their problem rather than my ineffectiveness."

Anger is the next emotion experienced in the dying process, and as a ministry dream begins to die, pastors likewise experience anger. Clergy are not immune to the irritability, touchiness, harsh words, or emotional outbursts associated with grief. In fact, some colleagues have been so vexed that upon exiting they refused to have a farewell party or greeting line. Sadly, their anger with certain members of the church kept them from accepting the appreciation of those who had been touched by their ministry.

Bargaining is the next stage most dying people experience. Similarly, many pastors have sought God's intervention in their crisis. Some pastors have also attempted to redefine expectations or renegotiate performance standards with the board. Some of them have tried to correct misunderstandings, strengthen deficiencies or just plain work harder. But once their chips were gone, rarely did positive results come from their working harder or trying to be someone they were not.

When a pastor can no longer deny, anger produces only greater reaction, and bargaining is ineffective, the phase of *depression* predictably follows. Depression expresses itself many ways, but very often the most obvious expression is withdrawal. In the words of one pastor, "There was no way I was going to reach out and care for a group of people who wanted me out of there!" Another said, "I was always a happy-go-lucky person and didn't really know what this solemnity was that had overcome me. I later learned it was depression." Mix loss of dreams, disillusionment with God's people, a sense of failure, and physical exhaustion, and you have a recipe for depression.

But, with time, clouds of discouragement begin to dissipate. Eventually, our eyes look up, and we see that the sun still shines, we still have marketable gifts, and God hasn't moved. The backward gaze of pain moves to a forward look of hope and acceptance. One pastor voiced it thus: "I still had some bitterness even about a year after the termination, but I came to understand that forgiveness is an act of the will. The feelings of hurt still come and go, but the anger and bitterness are gone." Another colleague knew that he had crossed over into the acceptance phase when he made this observation: "I was only getting paid eight dollars an hour at a temp job, yet I was deeply relieved that after working all day, I could go home without work and no phone calls. Unlike my previous people work, I was doing physical labor, and I could see at the end of the day what I had accomplished. And at that stage of my recovery, this was deeply satisfying."

Upon ordination, pastors do not become superhuman. The emotional spectrum for clergy is the same as it is for everyone else. Giving oneself permission to experience the natural emotions that flow from this life situation facilitates healing for the minister who is leaving vocational service.

A second analogy of the transition process is *the Exodus experience.* William Bridges describes each personal or institutional transition as a three-phase process.[3] At one end of his model is the beginning phase; at the other end is the ending phase. In between is what he calls *the wilderness.* He borrows heavily from the imagery of the Israelites' leaving Egypt, moving through the wilderness, and entering Canaan.

A new beginning actually starts in the ending phase of the previous job. Problems or restlessness usually surface before one's actual departure. People often check out even before they have left a job. Likewise, they still carry into the future with them pieces of the former situation.

Therefore, you shouldn't expect to get through any transition too quickly, especially the change from church service to marketplace employment. Rushing through the wilderness to enter a promised land is not necessarily healthful. On the other hand, lingering in the wilderness too long can likewise be unproductive. Although it is somewhat unsettling, the in-between period is a great time for self-assessment and focused preparation for a significant new beginning.

The flying trapeze is a third analogy for the transition process. Picture a rigging fifty feet in the air with platforms and trapeze at each end. Simply stated, a job change is releasing from one trapeze, flying briefly through the air, and then attaching firmly to the new trapeze. Obviously, although the image is easy to follow, the actual execution is much more intimidating for a pastor. Unlike acrobats, who practice this move extensively, a pastor is usually a novice regarding flying to a new vocation.

Releasing from a present trapeze is easier when you have some control over timing. If you can see another trapeze coming toward you, and if a safety net is beneath you, it is easier to release. Pastors who stay too long in their present ministry usually do so because they are unsure of where to go and because they have no security for the interim. Obviously, the worst case scenario is when someone else pries your fingers off the trapeze and releases you without another option, or safety net.

A national survey revealed that only 40 percent of pastors receive a severance package after forced termination.[4] Three months' salary was most often provided, although the range tends to increase with pastoral tenure, the size of the congregation, and the professional composition of its constituency. Since a typical job search can last three to fifteen months, pastors moving from congregation to marketplace should establish an interim financial net as soon as possible and begin looking for other trapeze options as quickly as they are able.

In summary, the themes of *movement* and *direction* are common across these three analogies. Endings happen. Sometimes we desire them; other times they are forced upon us. Bringing vocational and emotional closure can't be artificially rushed. At the same time, however, directional progress must continually be made. To live in denial, remain in Egypt, or clutch our current trapeze is pointless. To stay in depression, the wilderness, or free fall is likewise harmful. But if we keep making directional progress, regardless of the speed, then eventually we can know the joy of acceptance, the fruit of the Promised Land, and the exhilaration of the new trapeze.

A New Beginning

So how do we best move toward a new job? What steps should we follow? What practices are most helpful? Again, the counsel of those who have gone before us can help our transition into the market-place. Following is their collective wisdom.

Know yourself. Career consultants believe that a good job fit is one that has a 60–70 percent overlap between who you are and what the job requires. Therefore, for long-term satisfaction, a good vocational choice requires comprehensive self-awareness. Becoming a student of yourself means that you examine your personal D.E.P.T.H.:

*   *Desires:* What are your passions, dreams, and interests?
*   *Experience:* What accomplishments generate a sense of personal fulfillment?
*   *Personality:* How has God wired you psychologically?
*   *Talents:* What are your outstanding natural talents and learned skills?
*   *Holy Spirit:* How has the Holy Spirit gifted and led you in special ways?

Self-understanding is just as critical to the job hunt as networking with contacts and interviewing with perspective employers. The more diligently and professionally you attend to this area, the greater your self-awareness and therefore your job-search focus.

Utilize a team approach. For years, you have preached the importance of community and body life. You have affirmed the *one anothers* in Scripture. You have admonished people to use their gifts in serving others. Now it's time to accept your own advice and allow others to minister to you.

A good transition team is comprised of family, friends, a faith community, and a transition coach. Although the transition process can be painful for the minister, it may be more painful for his or her *family.* At least the pastor was present in board meetings, active in job decisions, and hearing concerns first hand. Too often, the spouse hears things second hand and feels helpless. Special care must be given to the unsettled world of a spouse and children. Family members need to be there for each other, allowing the change to draw them together rather then drive them apart. Husband, wife, and children more than ever need the support of one another as they move through the wilderness phase.

Friends are extremely important at this time. Some of your friendships may go back in time. One colleague affirmed, "It's helpful to keep in touch with people to whom you have ministered in the past. Years later, you will still appreciate these friendships." But some of our friends are in the congregation that we're leaving. Past ministerial ethics would advise to end all relationships upon exiting the congregation (whether it was a happy ending or a forced termination).

Today, personal friendships presumably will continue, even after the role relationship ends. The key here is to *ensure that you are not isolated*, advised one pastor. *Keep close to advisors,* said another. And a third stated, *Your friends need to give you honest feedback.* Colleagues warn us, however, that we must be careful to enjoy the mutual fellowship of church friends but not to use them for venting or counsel related to church matters.

A *faith community* is also essential for a healthful transition. God wired humanity for community. His design for your personal well-being, and that of others, is that you remain connected to people. Some pastors who move into the marketplace are able to remain within their present congregation, particularly where their exiting was not divisive. But in situations of tension or a forced termination, the clergy family had best find another church community.

Initially, a pastor in pain might not even want to go to church. One friend who knows the pain involved gave this warning: "Avoid doing TV church. You may hear some good preaching, but that's not the same as fellowship." Typically, your family will want to try several churches. However, as soon as possible, you will want to affiliate with one fellowship. As you are honest with the pastor, hopefully the church will see itself as a recovery center. The new minister can give pastoral care. Members can be instrumental in providing contacts for vocational guidance. And if the family has relocated geographically, the church can provide a hospitality role, assisting the family with housing and community connections (banking, power company, schools, etc.).

Finally, a good *transition counselor* can help with assessments, personal development and job networking. More will be said about this later, but for now we need to avoid the pride of going it alone. A team approach is the only way to thrive in a vocational wilderness.

Be diligent. God created the Sabbath for our benefit. Times of rest and change of pace are important for refreshing the soul. So after a season of intense ministry, especially where conflict may have been present, it's appropriate to take some "down time" for replenishing our physical, mental, and emotional reserves. A successful interview rarely takes place when a candidate is still bitter or angry, lacks self-worth, or is not feeling confident.

However, those who have made the transition into a new career warn against lapsing into slothfulness. In the words of one colleague, "Get off the couch!" The in-between jobs phase is neither a vacation nor retirement. Intentionality and focus are essential to an effective job search. One former pastor described his game plan thus: "Every day I read something about the field I was trying to enter. My wife and I met weekly with a counselor. Every other week I saw a vocational counselor. I also regularly scheduled appointments with people who could prove influential in my job search."

As we move through the recovery process, we must intentionally do the homework necessary for redirection. The adage is appropriate here: *Keep starting—and finishing will take care of itself.*

Be willing to accept interim employment. In only a few cases did the former pastors I interviewed find a new career in their first job. Most needed interim employment while they worked their networks. One colleague noted, "Initially, I was underemployed, but we could make it because of my wife's job and savings." Another minister explained it thus: "We put all options on the table. I knew I had to get going again, and I felt I was more marketable from a current position, even if I hadn't been there a long time."

Regarding initial or interim employment, it is also wise to hold a balanced perspective. One friend warns, "If you delay the transition process because you are looking for 'it,' you'll be disappointed." However, just jumping into anything to be working isn't wise either. You will be most happy serving in an area that capitalizes on your strengths, even if it is an interim situation. Another friend's admonition is a good summary: "Set your expectations realistically. You may try two or three things before you find what is right, before you discover what you can do with confidence."

Work and expand your networks. Of the twenty-five former pastors I interviewed, only one indicated that he found his new job through the want ads. In a few situations, professional employment agencies were helpful. But in most situations, reemployment was the result of a personal contact. I asked, "How did you find a new job?" One pastor responded, "I knew somebody." Another replied, "Through a person that I knew." A third stated, "On the recommendation of a friend."

Sometimes the connection was a member of the church or former church. Sometimes a job was found through a contact of a contact. And in a couple of cases it was from a third-level connection. In one situation, for example, the former pastor met with a ministry friend who introduced him to a business friend at a breakfast meeting. Later, that businessman introduced him to another businessman with whom this individual eventually found employment. The bottom line is that you must continually work your networks, giving them updates of your employment status and goals.

Pursue further training. No doubt you've heard these two sayings: "Knowledge is power" and "If you quit learning, you quit leading." Employers in the corporate world are hiring with laser precision. They can't afford any barnacles on their payrolls. And in every field, the learning curve keeps rising.

Some pastors found a job in the corporate world because of their current expertise. Perhaps it was people management, writing abilities, counseling, or program planning. More often, however, further training was required to bring one up to speed in a new field.

One pastor shared this story: "I always enjoyed working on my computer. I'd even taken a couple of classes in computer programming. With a little more training, I was able to take advantage of an opportunity that came my way." Another minister related, "I really enjoyed the pastoral care and counseling part of my former role. While I had taken counseling courses, I was not credentialed. I used my time after the pastorate to pursue the formal training and supervision that I needed to move into counseling."

For other people, the additional training was less formal. In the words of one associate, "I went to a number of business seminars to

see what the corporate world was discussing and what they were looking for. After a particular seminar on 'Business in the Twenty-first
Century,' I met with a number of leaders to discuss career options."

Whether through informal reading programs, classes, or seminars,
further training may be a prerequisite for a new job, as well as a requirement for advancement in that career.

Practice interview skills. Before actually interviewing for a job it's
important to understand the interviewing process. Books and videos
on interviewing and salary negotiations are available in libraries or for
purchase. In addition, some career coaches provide training in this
area, even videotaping and discussing your simulated interviews.

Although you do not want to jump into an interview unprepared,
waiting until you feel completely confident is not good either. One
pastor related, "I interviewed with nonprofits, and I interviewed with
businesses. The very process of listening to their questions and hearing my responses helped me become more articulate in subsequent
interviews." Personally, I don't endorse interviewing for interviewing sake. You need intentionality and focus in your job hunt. Nevertheless, the very process of interviewing can be a valuable learning
tool in building your confidence.

In the interview, be honest, realistic, and positive. If you don't
believe that you can make a contribution to the company, neither will
the interviewers be convinced. So have confidence in your God-wiring
and the skills that you have developed. One pastor said, "The
transferable skills of ministers are numerous. They have people skills
and expertise in project management and leadership. But that's not
what companies advertise they are looking for. You need to get into
the interview and show them what you can do." If you've studied the
company well and know what they are looking for, you can show
how your skills transfer, helping their bottom line.

Care for your family along the way. A job transition is a family transition, and family dishevelment is especially acute for the clergy family
moving from a professional ministry marketplace. Chapter 16 provides more information about helping the family in the transition process, so a simple reminder is appropriate for now.

A couple's response to this transition depends on the nature of the crisis, personal culpability, personality, previous patterns of interaction, and other contextual variables. Some couples have found their marriage strained during this wilderness experience. The personal pain of each led to withdrawal into private worlds, with occasional blaming or critical remarks. For example, one pastor admitted, "I was so hurt by the church that I simply got out of there. I left the state and moved in with our in-laws until the family could join me. I was so overwhelmed with my own personal pain that I failed to be there for her with the pain she was going through."

Other couples have shared that their termination brought them closer together. Time spent with a counselor and time spent together in daily prayer allowed their relationship to deepened in spite of the uncertainty at the time.

In certain situations, the ministry partner can be more victimized by the change and grieves leaving the church more than the minister does. Part of his or her identity is also being lost. One former pastor shared regretfully, "I was a good pastor, and my wife was an excellent pastor's wife. I'm no longer a pastor because of a poor decision I made. But she is no longer a pastor's wife, not because of anything she did but because of my choice. And it pains me to see her out of her ministry context because of my failure."

Regardless of the reasons underlying the change from professional career service, caring for your family is a top priority in the transition journey.

Maintain hope. All of the pastors whom I interviewed eventually made a successful career transition. A few have chosen to reenter vocational Christian service; however, most of them have preferred to remain in their marketplace employment. They have discovered that they can use their gift mix and have enjoyed their less-pressured role in the church as a volunteer.

These feelings, however, weren't present early in the transition process. Many of them voiced concern about making it in the business world. One pastor expressed it thus: "Other than part-time jobs during college, I had never worked in any setting but the church. I wasn't sure I had what it took to swim with the sharks in the corporate world."

These colleagues were pleasantly surprised, however, to find that people valued them and expressed appreciation for their contributions. One former minister observed, "It was a huge relief for me to know that I could cut it in the average job market. I was surprised that my ministry skills served me well in the secular marketplace." Another shared, "The first few months on the job, I was wondering whether I'd even be able to learn to do this. But as I look back, I can see how the Lord actually prepared me for the transition to this particular job. And now I have fun each day doing what I am doing, and I'm successful at it."

One advantage Christians have in the secular marketplace is that they're not working primarily for an employer but rather for Christ. One former pastor observed, "One thing that I found in the corporate work place is that there are a lot of slackers out there. If I worked hard, I distinguish myself in the eyes of others." Another colleague discovered, "The first job that I took had so many people just marking time that I began to shine just simply because I showed up and did my job. I thought incompetence existed in the church; in the public sector it seems to increase exponentially!" Your Christian work ethic and your skill set makes you extremely valuable to employers.

Summary

Can there be life after the pastorate? Of course! Even after an ugly forced termination? For sure! Not only is there hope for a successful career transition for a pastor moving into the marketplace but also the corporate world is replete with real ministry possibilities. As one colleague put it, "Many opportunities for ministry exist in the marketplace, perhaps even more than in the church. Real people are out there with real needs and are not afraid to admit it. In addition, there are many good Christians out there to partner with us in ministry."

In reality, there is no job field that a person can enter today that is guaranteed to be there at retirement. Each year, thousands of jobs evaporate, and new types of work develop. The idea of life-long employment in one job, let alone one field, is no longer expected. However, although no particular job can offer security, gifted, hard-working individuals with developed passions and skills will always be secure.

They are their own security because God wired them with a gift mix that will always be valuable to the right employer. Our responsibility, whether we are working in the church or the marketplace, is to labor in the environment that best matches our creation design. When we do so, we will find personal fulfillment, be able to care for our families, and touch other lives for Christ's kingdom.

14

WHEN YOU WANT TO MOVE, BUT NO ONE'S KNOCKING

ALL OF US KNOW PASTORS WHO WANT TO move but feel stuck. We have lived there ourselves; perhaps a number of you are there right now. Maybe some of you that are reading this book have even jumped directly to this chapter, hoping to discover a quick pathway to relocation. Unfortunately, quick fixes, especially in church service, do not exist. As one career consultant admits, "Moving within the church is the most difficult movement in the professional world. The typical pastor I run into is frustrated, and it is the same theme: 'I've been here too long; I don't know where else to move.'"[1]

Research reveals that one of eight ministers is thinking of resigning.[2] The percentage of those who would like a change but are not that desperate is probably even higher. An editor of a magazine for ministers once told me, "John, I hope your book has some answers . . . of all the phone calls I receive from pastors, the number one problem they express is feeling trapped in their church."

Diverse role expectations, the weight of people's problems, family pressures, mismatch of fit, and exhausting service in the absence of appreciation all cause relocation to look attractive. Making a good move is tough, however. We've seen the parched grass in some other parishes, and, frankly, we're not that hungry. Even if we are willing to take an unhealthy church, supply and demand is currently on the side of congregations. Search committees get as many as one hundred resumes for their positions. Furthermore, like it or not, churches discriminate in hiring: many churches prefer men over women, married over single, and younger over those who are older than fifty.

So what's a minister to do to get unstuck? Is there any hope? Most certainly! Thousands of churches are contacting pastors daily. Hundreds of churches are extending calls. "Over ninety percent of the pastors who want to find a church, including those who experienced involuntary termination, are placed eventually," remarks a career counselor. The process is not easy; it takes hard work. But by gaining perspective, increasing our value, and strengthening our support networks, we raise our relocation chances significantly.

Gaining Perspective

Some pastors seeking a ministry change enjoy their church, yet they would like to leave on a high note. Most of those who are hoping for relocation, however, feel unappreciated, unfulfilled, and, in extreme cases, completely spent. A district minister warns, "When pastors find themselves being defensive, standoffish, developing an exclusive spirit, an insensitive unapproachable style, they need to seriously address their situation." Taking time to gain perspective is the first step in regaining control.

Checking our emotional resources. If we find ourselves drained of coping resources and unable to handle congregational pressure points, the last thing we should think about is relocation. Seeking to escape may just complicate our problems. "Taking any church just because you want to work in the church is just as bad as deciding to make pornography just because you want to eat. You won't do the ministry there well, and people will suffer, all in the name of your vocation. You certainly have the right to suffer for your own vocation but no right to cause others to suffer for it."[3] Jumping at any opening just because we're emotionally exhausted is an unwise move.

A more healthful way to begin is by processing how we feel, analyzing our situation, studying alternatives, and planning how we can gain strength. Prayer, especially with spouse or confidant, is helpful. Counseling with a professional pastoral counselor is likewise productive. Even journaling gets us moving outward, as one colleague discovered: "I did some writing, just for my own benefit, trying to get my confused thoughts down on paper. And as I did that, I tried to process what I was feeling, evaluate my present ministry, and think about what made me happy and unhappy. As a result of the journaling, I was able to work through that fairly difficult experience."

Becoming a student of yourself. God has stamped his mark of uniqueness on all of creation. Whether we look at snowflakes or faces, diversity is the norm. No one has our exact physiology. Even identical twins have their subtle differences. No two individuals have the same personality or temperament. Perfectly matched temperament profiles can't be found. Our uniqueness is further developed through the myriad experiences through which we alone walk. It is fashioned by talents and giftedness. Before we consider a job change, then, it makes sense to study our uniqueness.

Arthur F. Miller relates our uniqueness to employment thus:

> Issues of job search, job fit, and career direction, are prematurely addressed until the person comes to an accurate and complete understanding of what the Bible calls his "ways" or mode of action (Jeremiah 17:10; 2 Chronicles 6:30; 1 Kings 8:39; Job 34:11; Ezekiel 18:30; Proverbs 5:21). You possess a mode of action, a distinct 'way' of operating when you are at your most productive and most fulfilled. You have repeatedly used certain abilities; concentrated on certain subjects or objects; required certain structure, visibility, standards, outcome and conditions; functioned in a certain relationship with others; and achieved a certain payoff of precious personal significance.[4]

Dozens of books (such as those in the endnotes) can guide your self-awareness inquiry. Many of them are available in local bookstores or community lending libraries. In addition, specific diagnostic instruments can actually map our talents, skills, impact styles, enthusiasms, and even ministry interests.

The very process of developing self-understanding moves us in a productive direction. That direction may even surprise us: "Having inventoried our gifts, even if we end up staying in that parish, reinvigorates our ministry. We see finally what we love to do, and we can call in others in the congregation to take over parts we don't like."[5] Whether we move or stay, becoming a student of ourselves strengthens our shepherding.

Reevaluating expectations. At the heart of many pastor/people conflicts lie unrealistic expectations. Naiveté resides among many congregants; they have no comprehension of ministry demands. When leadership fails to define and communicate ministry priorities, members ascribe their own hierarchy and demands to the job. These multiple and often divergent expectations can overwhelm a pastor.

Ministers, however, are also susceptible to unrealistic expectations. As one executive minister observes, "Some pastors have simply never established a positive track record. They have had marginal proficiencies, attitudinal problems, they can't preach, and maybe they are plain lazy." Intel does not retain a marginal performer; AT&T does not accept ineptness. Why would a pastor ever think that a congregation should tolerate mediocrity?

Another unrealistic expectation relates to employment in general. Richard Bolles puts it thus: "People often see vocational contentment as a happy match between what you have to do and what you enjoy doing. But there is no such permanent match. When you define contentment as an ideal match, which I did for years, you are subject to the fact that it is like a passion: it often doesn't last long. But when you define contentment as the ability to let God transform your job, then you'll find contentment."[6]

A desire to relocate may be an attempt to find a quick way to escape the demands of a congregation. Unrealistically high or diverse expectations on the part of the people kindle our desire to leave; misunderstanding regarding contentment fuels the fire. Reality testing of expectations, with objective help when possible, identifies the source(s) toward which to direct remedial efforts.

Refusing comparison. Sometimes feeling stuck in a church might have more to do with envy than with expectations. The church-growth movement and the notoriety of megachurches have left many general practitioners of smaller churches feeling unimportant. A desire to lead a multiple staff, preach to a larger crowd, or even move to the sunbelt can foster discontent with our present situation.

But hoping that a better situation will bring satisfaction sets us up for disappointment. One colleague noted this example: "There is pressure on a ministry in mid-life to get a bigger church because of financial demands (kids going to college, etc.), but reality teaches that many pastors will not likely move to a bigger church. They have aspirations that in reality cannot be fulfilled. Some even feel, 'I deserve better; I've worked hard!'"

By refusing comparison, we are free to give our best efforts to our own people. Fantasizing about other congregations only weakens our present ministry marriage.

Broadening our horizons. Many pastors do not have a life outside of their church. Although we must abhor the hireling syndrome (seeing the ministry as just a job), we must equally avoid the opposite extreme of allowing the work to consume us. Unlike other jobs, there is very little closure in pastoral ministry. Preach your best sermon, and another one is due in a week. Listen attentively to a counselee, and a dozen more are waiting for an appointment. Visit newcomers, the sick, and shut-ins, and additional names join the list. The cycle never ends. But for the sake of freshness, wholeness, and balance, we must add some variety into our routines; we must punctuate our schedules with needed changes of pace.

Our life is more than the church. We are refreshed by friends, hobbies, and other extracurricular activities. Whether we are overwhelmed or underchallenged in our present ministry, developing interests beyond the congregation expands and refreshes us. One counselor recommended self-exercises through other ministry avenues: "Pastors frustrated over the slower pace of their lay leaders might explore additional ministries such as police or hospital chaplaincies. Pastors with a gift for writing might turn their sermons into pamphlets and books. Some pastors find great fulfillment in teaching at a local Christian school or even secular institutions. Such ministries help the pastor cope with feelings of a distorted pastoral role—too much time working at administration and soothing ruffled feathers, not enough time exercising his spiritual gifts."[7]

Obviously, balance is required when participating in extra-congregational activities. Pastors have hurt their reputations by overinvestment in a counseling practice, landscaping business, or writing career. Yet, a modest involvement in outside activities provides experiences and strokes that make us less vulnerable to the changing feelings of the membership. Our improved attitude and strength of character, in turn, offer the church stronger leadership.

Being stuck doesn't have to mean being stagnant. The frustration of wanting to move because we are underchallenged is diminished as we responsibly broaden our horizons.

Trusting God's sovereignty. Taking time to gain perspective must always include trusting God's sovereignty. Isn't it funny how we can know something in our head but struggle to transfer it to our feelings? How often have we referenced Romans 8:28, and how many times have we quoted, "Trust in the Lord with all your heart and lean not on your own understanding; in all your ways acknowledge him and he will make your paths straight" (Prov. 3:5–6)? Yet, let's admit it, when it comes to a ministry move, we are agitated by God's silence.

God is the shaper of our personality, the supplier of our giftedness, and the opener and closer of doors. While we are free to network and make things happen, we can also rest in His timetable. The process of transforming us into *the full measure of the stature of Christ* may include delaying our move. One colleague shared this example: "We certainly learned during those months to trust the sovereignty of God, although we were not always cheerful and joyful amid the trial. God taught us a lot about ourselves and about what He called us to do and had not called us to do. As a result, I think we were strengthened for our future ministry." Meditating on God's sovereignty yields peace, even amid uncertainty.

The saying is true: "It's hard to put out a fire if you are standing in the middle of it." When one is dealing with some situations, backing away is imperative. But when we feel the heat in church ministry, escape is not our only choice. Moving to a new congregation may eventually be the best solution, but we cannot be sure until we first back away to gain perspective. By checking emotional resources, becoming a student of ourselves, reevaluating expectations, refusing comparison, broadening our horizons, and trusting God's sovereignty, we take the first step in getting unstuck.

Increasing Our Value

I once heard someone say, "If you want to be loved more, be more loveable, and if you want to be more loveable, be more valuable." Career counselors would advise something similar: "If you want to become more marketable, become more valuable."

Becoming more valuable makes pastors more attractive to any congregation, including their own. One colleague phrased it thus: "On the practical side about marketability, I think it's important to realize that churches are looking for pastors who are happy where they are. They want them to be productive, satisfied and growing— not discontent. If a pastor is unhappy, a whole range of issues are raised that they want to pursue. So to improve marketability, a minister needs to honestly express some degree of contentment with the present church." By blooming where we're planted, we strengthen our current work and increase our desirability to churches looking for a pastor.

Taking personal care. In the press of the church service, too often self-care is low on the list of priorities. Although we know how intricately woven are the physical, emotional, relational, and spiritual dimensions of our lives, we still neglect personal disciplines. Surveys reveal that pastors spend insufficient time in prayer and devotional study, yet we know that the congregation is fed from the overflow of our spiritual reservoir. Psychologists stress the importance of close relationships, yet we seldom know intimacy. Health professionals remind us of the importance of rest, exercise, and proper nutrition, yet some colleagues are dangerously out of shape.

Enough is enough. Let's get with it! As we pay more attention to ourselves, we begin to feel better about ourselves, and the congregation will also feel better about us. The area where most pastors should begin is with regular exercise. Cardiovascular improvement and muscle toning can be accomplished by simply walking briskly for twenty-five minutes three to four times a week. People who exercise consistently tend automatically to watch what they eat. Obviously, we need to limit rich foods, but pounds will come off when we simply eat in moderation while maintaining an exercise regimen. The energy, stamina, and spiritual and emotional reserves needed for people ministry increase as we get in shape.

We've heard the expression, *The teacher IS the message*, meaning that who we are communicates more than what we say. Becoming more valuable, therefore, requires addressing our person along with the practice of our ministry.

Become more knowledgeable. Too often, pastors fall into the temptation of doing the same thing, same song, same procedures and approach, all of the time, without being creative. Yet, professionals who are not keeping up with developments in their field are working on borrowed time. One colleague put it thus: "Growing churches require growing pastors. The moment the pastor stops growing, so does the church. All leaders are learners. The moment I stop learning, I stop leading."[8] Perhaps if we're in a dead end in our career, it's because we drove into that cul-de-sac and turned off the key years ago.

The Bible says that "we reap what we sow." Colleagues in obsolescence can't blame others. A plethora of resources is available for personal and professional growth. Seminars, workshops, books, videos, and periodicals provide insight on every ministry dimension. If we cannot afford a subscription to *Pastor to Pastor*[9] or *Audio-Tech Business Book Summaries*,[10] we can still receive free conference summaries and briefings from organizations such as Leadership Network.[11] Some pastors co-op resources with other colleagues. In addition, public lending libraries loan materials by Ken Blanchard, Gary Hamel, Robert Kaplan, Daniel Coleman, John Kotter, Michael Hammer, John Naisbitt, and other secular leadership gurus. Although everything that these authors write is not applicable, it's all stretching. In addition to providing material from which we can glean insights, these writers familiarize us with the environments in which many of our congregants work. Whether we read a book or attend a conference, listen to a tape or begin a Doctor of Ministry program, becoming more knowledgeable increases our value to a congregation.

Nurturing enthusiasm, offering hope, becoming an encourager. Ministers who feel pressed to the wall usually see the problem people, not the faithful workers; they dwell on the unfinished tasks, not the recent accomplishments. But if we can push out of the corner enough to gain perspective, to start caring for ourselves, and to revive learning, we may start noticing the roses in the church, not just the thorns. A positive outlook increases enthusiasm, and genuine enthusiasm (not shallow optimism) is contagious.

Christians have Christ's companionship in ministry (Matt. 8:20), are "equipped for every good work" (2 Tim. 3:17), and are able to do "all things through Him" (Phil. 4:13 NASB), the Provider of strength. Even in the midst of difficult circumstances, we have grounds for genuine optimism.

Recently, I heard a seminar leader state, "The person who offers the most hope carries the most authority." People are not interested in following pastors who themselves are overwhelmed by problems. If I am drowning, I want to latch onto someone who can drag me toward shore—not someone who'll pull me under. People caught on the barbed wire of life are looking for hope.

Whether you call it the cut, jab, dig, or rip, the art of piercing another person with words has been perfected in our generation. But doesn't it feel good to receive a thoughtful word, an expression of kindness, or a note of encouragement? How appreciative we are when we learn from a third party about someone's saying something nice about us. Building up and encouraging another person is not a cheap strategy for gaining approval. These practices flow naturally from the heart of a believer who is touched by Christ's love. But a by-product of encouragement is appreciation. As we minister in the power of the God of hope, offering genuine and generous encouragement, we become more valuable.

Strengthening ministry practices. Closely related to becoming more knowledgeable is the development of fundamental pastoral skills. Preaching, for example, can be strengthened through more careful exegesis, better familiarization with pulpit notes, and a more focused application. Evaluating ourselves on video or having others evaluate us can prove helpful. A sermon checksheet with items such as pulpit manners, clarity of message, diction, use of illustrations, application to life, and other factors are included in most preaching textbooks.

Giving focused attention to managerial tasks improves our service. Conducting a time audit (noting our activity every fifteen minutes) is helpful. Working ahead of due dates reduces stress and usually delivers a better product. Giving priority items (the important versus the urgent) our greatest attention reaps the highest yield.

Increasing the scope and depth of care-giving also expands the value of our ministry. Jesus said, "I know my sheep and my sheep know me" (John 10:14). It's hard for a pastor sitting behind a desk to develop this kind of ministry with the flock. Each of us is capable of calling or visiting a few more people each week. Increased visibility is politically wise, but that's a side benefit. Greater involvement with people on their turf makes them more receptive to all of our ministry.

Paying attention to routine demeanor can also affect our ministry significantly. Good eye contact, careful listening, correct grammar, keeping our word, appropriate apparel, a warm smile, good posture, maintaining confidentialities, and thoroughness are just a few behaviors worth monitoring and improving.

Completing our legacy. Many pastors leave a church before maximizing their contribution. Sometimes personal problems or congregational frustrations have led to a stalled vision. A great time to rekindle that vision and complete our charge is when we want to move but are still awaiting direction.

Since leadership development is at the heart of our task (Eph. 4:11–13), a significant amount of our remaining time should be spent with those who will carry on the ministry in our absence. Key players can help plan worship, become involved in visitation, co-lead Bible studies, and strategize for the future. Leaving the church in the hands of a competent laity is a great contribution.

Colleagues desiring to move should ask, "If I had only twelve more months with the congregation, what would I want to accomplish?" Whether it's developing a volleyball outreach, a couples retreat ministry, or a children's club program, our efforts can make our remaining time more fulfilling and leave the church with a richer legacy.

Strengthening Support Networks

When I was a child, my grandmother rebuked my timidity: "Johnny, never be afraid to ask for help." Over the years, I've experienced the wisdom of her words. Pastoral counselors offer the same advice when one is facing the need for a move: "As in all the other lonely places where clergy may find themselves, the sagest advice is to resist the temptation to deal with these matters alone. In the midst of great tension and conflict, our judgment is apt to be constricted and even impaired. And the heat and confusion and embarrassment of big trouble, one may be reluctant to ask others for help."[12] "Don't go it alone!" is the repetitive advise we hear from those who have experienced job transition.

God is the anchor of our support network. The size of our support team will vary, but the most important Player never changes: God is the provider of peace (Phil. 4:7) and the lord of circumstances (Rom. 8:28). Without Him, we can do nothing (John 15:5); with Him, we can do all things (Phil. 4:13). As we meet Him in the pages of Scripture, commune with Him through prayer, and rejoice in Him through worship, our hope for the future is increased. The God who gives us every good and perfect gift (James 1:17), who allows us to call Him *Abba, Father* (Rom. 8:15), and who knows the number of the hairs on our head (Luke 12:7) also has our best interest in hand (John 10).

Family members are the primary players on the transition team. Crises rarely affect only one individual. The family of the pastor who feels stuck also feels the frustration. Unfortunately, family members don't always pull together during times of crises; sometimes they act adversarial under pressure. Disagreements may escalate; blaming is not uncommon.

No matter how great the pressure, emotional resources must be focused against the dilemma. Rather than viewing one another as the problem, we must pull together toward resolution. When a family member is ready to quit, the rest of the family must patiently encourage. One of my friends has in the parsonage a drawing of a young couple leaning against each other and holding hands. The caption reads, "You and me against the world." As allies, we can meet any challenge.

Fellow pastors are a critical piece of our support network. Many times when I was driving through Westville, New Jersey, I would stop to see Harry. Although I had a close relationship with several folks in our church, some things can only be appreciated by another minister. Together, we experienced the catharsis of humor, discussion, and prayer. Clergy understand the weight of the ministry, they personally experience church tensions, and most of them have dealt with implementing congregational change. Colleagues are important to our emotional well-being; they provide stability and hope.

Influential pastors may serve as nominators. The dilemma of preachers is that they do not have a Yenta to match-make a church for them. They are like the kid who sits at the edge of the dance floor wishing he had a partner with whom to dance but simply waiting for someone to ask him. "Unfortunately," admits this pastor friend, "many wait and wait, without ever being asked." Ministers who do get asked are often those who are recommended by an influential colleague. These nominators are usually pastors of significant churches or well-known teachers in the denomination. Names they give to a search committee will likely be investigated further. An out-of-the-blue call to a leader whom we do not know will probably be ignored. But a cordial conversation during a conference or the passing of our name to them through a mutual friend can generate some leads.

Denominational leaders can make strategic contacts. For pastors who are serving within denominations, state coordinators, district superintendents and national officers are good sources of referral. Obviously, they are more eager to recommend someone whom they've observed in ministry and have seen active in the denomination. These executives are also more interested in placing a minister with a good track record than one who has a problematic history.

District executives are a resource for both pastors and churches. Unfortunately, since pastors come and go while churches remain, some superintendents sense a pressure to side with the congregation when conflicts arise. For this reason, it is wise to lean on friends and colleagues for venting frustrations and the district executives for relocation networking.

Placement services are a growing source for referrals. For decades pastors have contacted placement offices at Bible colleges and seminaries regarding church positions that have been posted with their institutions. Christian schools remain an excellent resource for ministry possibilities. However, today, hundreds of congregations advertise their ministry openings directly on the Web, using Internet placement services such as churchstaffing.org and ministersearch.com. Personally submitting a resume to a church used to be taboo. Today, an electronic resume submitted in response to a Web posting is given an honest review.

Business professionals should be included in our network. People in the business world can give us a different window through which to view our current situation. Furthermore, they may open a door to secular employment. One colleague found transition work in a counseling service, another with a government agency; one entered the marketing field, and another joined a computer firm. Involuntary termination precipitated a couple of these career changes. A need for a radically different vocational climate initiated the others. Contacts with the business community can prove helpful during transition, even if only as intermediate employment.

Professional career counselors provide critical assistance. As soon as we sense the possible need for a new beginning, it's wise to seek professional career counseling. Career counselors can provide insight into ourselves and the type of job for which we are best suited. Career counselors do not focus on pathological problems; their goal is to "bring out awareness and appreciation of successes and achievements, strengths, skills, and competencies."[13] Second, they can shed light on the job-hunt process, what it takes to get hired. Some of their advice has been recorded in books that professionals have authored. When possible, however, we're better off meeting personally with a counselor for testing and processing.

Career counseling can cost anywhere from $1,500 to $3,000, but it's well worth the testing and consulting fee. Sometimes churches are willing to fund assessment expenses. But even when a church is not willing to pay and our own finances are squeezed, the personal benefits still outweigh the cost. This belief has led one colleague to argue, "Many people say they do not have the funds for counseling when they have assets, savings accounts, trust funds for children, and many kinds of things that have been either inherited or acquired through the years. . . . What I am saying is to look creatively at the possible resources you might have."[14] Career counselors are another indispensable part of a strong support network.

Who you know *is* important. If we haven't participated in ministerials, served on denominational committees, attended conferences, or initiated fellowship with colleagues, we're probably not well known. And since the hardest people to market are invisible people, whatever our participation level in the past, now is a good time to get involved in colleague groups.

Summary

A number of years ago, I invited a career counselor for breakfast to talk about getting unstuck. My impression before that meeting was that most pastors who were stuck in an invisible congregation, especially those pastors who have been fired, would probably not find another church in which to serve. To my surprise, he disclosed that just the opposite occurs: "People who really feel 'called' usually do find another church. Their transition period may take longer than desired, but the far majority seeking relocation eventually get unstuck."

So what do we do when an analysis of transition signals suggests that we're free to leave or when crises force a move? First, we must not withdraw but get advice. Second, we must not give up but persist. By following the game plan for gaining perspective, increasing our value, and strengthening support networks, we maximize our marketability. Finding our next place of service, then, is just down the road.

15

PREPARING THE CHURCH
FOR A PASTORAL TRANSITION

A MINISTER'S GOAL NEAR THE CLOSE OF A pastorate is to release the congregation to soar on its own. Yes, a new leader will eventually be called. But in interim the congregation must minister passionately, not just coast until a new pastor arrives. Therefore, even as you make plans to leave, you will want to prepare the church for its next chapter by affirming them and releasing them. A good *good-bye* completes your contribution to their well-being.

No matter where on the personal satisfaction continuum you would place your congregation, a cordial farewell will bring strength to the church, wholeness to you and your family, and honor to God. Whatever the breadth of your contribution, your legacy is enriched when the congregation is left with a positive resignation, permission to grieve, preaching that inspires hope, counsel for transitional leadership, information helpful to the next pastor, and a gracious and final release.

A Positive Resignation

The morning service we attended as visitors was truly uplifting. Worship was inspiring, and the message was insightful and well delivered. What a rare privilege to encounter this type of experience while on vacation! The bomb hit after the sermon when the pastor said, "Before the benediction, there is something I need to say to you," and then he proceeded to read his letter of resignation. Apparently, this man's tenure at the church had not been easy. We didn't have to know the details to sense his disappointment with the resistance to his leadership. Several minutes later, a quiet congregation filed out of the auditorium. Some people were hurt, some were angry, some were confused, and some were disbelieving. One thing they had in common was that they all had forgotten the worship and the sermon once *the bomb* was dropped.

A good transition begins with a healthful, edifying resignation. Rather than shocking the congregation with an announcement from the pulpit, many pastors have found it beneficial to notify the members in writing. A letter mailed on Monday morning will reach most congregants by Wednesday. People will then have several days to process their feelings before hearing any public statement. This procedure also provides time to notify key leaders and close friends personally while the letters are en route. One colleague who followed this procedure said, "By Sunday, the entire congregation knew, and when they met me at the church it was like, 'There's Bob—he's leaving, you know.'" By the time an outgoing pastor meets the congregation corporately, an acceptance of the situation is already developing.

Most congregants will read a pastor's letter of resignation more than once. Because of the letter's significance, its words must be skillfully crafted. Following are the characteristics of a healthful resignation letter.

It focuses on the positive. In even the most difficult of ministries, many contributions have been made to people's lives. Therefore, a barbed, vindictive resignation letter is never appropriate. One pastor commented sadly, "During almost twenty-two years on a presbytery staff and as a Presbyterian executive, I spent countless hours repairing the damage of destructive good-byes to both congregations and pastors."[1] Since the future of the pastor and the church begins with this important statement of closure, an upbeat resignation gets them both moving in the right direction.

It communicates the difficulty of our choice. All of us are uneasy as we approach the intersection of transition. The regulatory signals studied earlier illustrate the complexity of making a wise choice. The congregation is helped by knowing that leaving was not an easy decision. People are more understanding of an individual who admits having struggled with discerning God's leading.

It expresses appreciation. A positive resignation letter expresses appreciation to the congregation and acknowledges pastoral leadership as both a trust and a privilege. We have been allowed to choose hymns, select leaders, determine preaching passages, touch the needy, and make a whole host of directional decisions. Even if some people have resisted this leadership, every minister has had an incredible opportunity to serve as an undershepherd of the Chief Shepherd. For this privilege, we must express thanks.

It affirms the journey together. Ministerial gains and successes do not come without the efforts of many people. Any strides made by the church during a pastor's tenure were a joint venture. Volunteers have contributed thousands of hours of service. The congregation's labors are always worth commending.

It offers hope. People are further encouraged by their pastor's belief that God has great plans ahead for the congregation. Jesus saw Peter in Cephas and Paul in Saul. Although people are not necessarily motivated by the image they see in the mirror, they will ignite with enthusiasm when presented with a vision of whom they can *become.* A good *good-bye* reminds the congregation that Jesus Christ is the Lord of all believers, and that He is just beginning to accomplish His work among them. Truly, He is able to do "immeasurably more than all [they] ask or imagine" (Eph. 3:20).

It explains the decision. A resignation letter should address the preeminent question in people's minds: "Why is the pastor leaving?" Failure to answer the *why* question leads to speculation and suspicion. These, in turn, lead to withdrawal, anger, and factionalism. Providing several clear-cut reasons for the decision facilitates understanding and healing.

Some congregants are comforted by a spiritual answer: "I believe I'm following God's leading." Others are more understanding when they learn that the decision was based on a matching of giftedness, the importance of being near family, or other practical reasons. A discussion of the whole decision-making process is overkill, but a list of three or four reasons why a call has been accepted helps people to adjust to the idea.

It denotes when you are leaving. People will want to know the effective date of the resignation. This gives perspective to the transition. Knowing that you will be around for a certain number of days assures people that they'll have an opportunity to say farewell and time to make important interim plans.

One pastor summarizes the resignation communication process thus: "A letter of resignation to the congregation needs to be a healing instrument and a statement of faith. It should convey a sense of God's sovereignty and be filled with hope. Being positive about joys and victories together can help the congregation be joyful over the past. Stating our sorrow at leaving but stating our commitment to obedience affirms we are making what we believe to be a right choice."[2] Because a positive resignation letter brings healthy closure for both pastor and people, it's the first step toward a new, healthy beginning.

Permission to Grieve

The crucifixion and resurrection of Jesus Christ was not totally unexpected. Several times before His arrest, Jesus predicted His death. Yet, even with the cross immediately before Him, His concern was for the well-being of His disciples. In the Upper Room, He demonstrated His love for them (John 13:1–12), promised them another comforter (John 14), painted a picture of their future fruitfulness (John 15), and prayed for all believers (John 17). Especially interesting to note is that Jesus promised them that their grief would turn to joy (John 16:19–24). Christ understood what today is called *grief work*.

We humans must grieve our losses; it's part of our creation design. Researchers in the field of death and dying have identified five ways in which people respond to loss, whether real or anticipated. Other people have confirmed that these reactions occur after losing a loved one, losing a job, or even losing a pastor.

In chapter 13, we described the grief process as it relates to a pastor's leaving vocational service. People losing their pastor will experience the same emotions (denial, anger, bargaining, depression, and acceptance). Individuals will move through these stages at various rates, but you should not be surprised to hear and see expressions of their loss.

The ending of a pastoral relationship is difficult for both congregation and cleric, whatever the circumstances. Although some ministers are happy to get out of there and some members are glad that they're leaving, most often there is also a sense of loss. Some folks may deny the finality of the decision or try to reverse it by bargaining. Others become angry, feeling betrayed by their trusted shepherd. Discouragement will convince some people that the future will never be as great as the past. But eventually, with enough time for closure and proper transition, most of the church family will move to the stage of acceptance, trusting that things will work out.

Pastors who are considering transition usually have a several-month head start over members regarding *grief work*. By listening to people and empathizing with their feelings, a departing pastor can help congregants catch up. Defensiveness, withdrawal, or anger on our part will prolong their grief. As we affirm the bargainer, accept the venting of the angered, and share a hug with the depressed, we contribute toward congregational healing. Eventually, as with Christ's disciples, their grief can turn to joy.

Preaching That Inspires Hope

"Dad, what's gonna happen to Betsy and me if you and Mom die?" That was the question our son asked when he was seven years old. A death in the congregation had triggered Ben's thoughts. He began to feel insecure, wondering what the future would hold.

When members of a church family learn of their pastor's resignation, some of those natural feelings arise. If you are leaving a congregation, your job is to give them hope for the future, or, in the words of a colleague, "To help people build confidence in themselves and in the Lord during our time of absence." This infusion of hope can take place through personal conversations as you let your confidence rub off on people. Corporately, it can happen through the crafting of your final sermons.

Preaching that inspires hope does the following things:

It avoids hostility. Pastors who shoot at people from the pulpit invariably wound themselves. No matter how unappreciative a congregation may have been, a shepherd who is concerned for the welfare of the flock never beats the sheep. Attacking your critics does not change their mind; more likely, you'll end up losing the respect of your supporters. In personal conversations and especially in public presentations, an outgoing pastor must resist the urge to prolong the battle.

It points to the future. Paul, after many great accomplishments, said, "Forgetting what is behind and straining toward what is ahead, I press on toward the goal to win the prize for which God has called me heavenward" (Phil. 3:13–14). Perhaps during your tenure, church membership doubled in size, neighborhood outreach flourished and several families were commissioned to the mission field. Even so, this might be just the beginning of greater things for the congregation. Preaching on God's goodness, faithfulness, and promises offers encouragement and hope.

It encourages service. Successful church programs are never the result of a solo performance. Without people working in the nursery and classrooms or reaching out in hospitality and visitation, ministry would stall. Just as the hand, foot, eye, and ear are all critical to the body's functioning, the ongoing health of a congregation is maintained only as members build up and encourage one another, bear each other's burdens, submit to those in authority, and practice servanthood. Preaching that reminds people of the joy of serving both the Lord and others strengthens the Christian community.

Counsel for Transitional Leadership

As a departing pastor, you should expect to provide counsel to those who will hold key positions of leadership in your absence. Your role is not to plan the interim workings of the church or set goals for the future but to be available as an advisor. Any minister who has poured vast amounts of time and energy into the congregation would be remiss in just walking away and leaving members without guidance. As one colleague reminds us, "It is better to leave the church in motion than to leave it stalled out."

Pastoral counsel is often needed (even if it is not requested) regarding the following issues.

Realignment of responsibilities. Whether the church has a remunerated multiple staff or only lay leaders, redefining of ministry descriptions is a must to ensure continuance of all pastoral functions. Preaching, care-giving, and administrative coordination will still be needed. Remember that a responsibility that is *everyone's* responsibility becomes *no one's* responsibility. Someone will have to visit absentees, compose the worship bulletin, and provide counseling. All ministry bases need coverage. Your suggestions on realignment possibilities will provide insight for the leadership.

Recommendations for competent pulpit supply. Immediately after your departure, the congregation would probably benefit from a variety of preaching styles. Although denominational executives, staff associates, or parachurch representatives can bring a freshness to the pulpit, continuity and predictability are also important. Absenteeism is higher when a smorgasbord preaching approach extends the twelve- to eighteen-month period that is typical of pastoral vacancies. After four to six weeks of guest speakers, most churches find it more productive to retain one interim preacher.

Large churches with a multiple staff and strong lay leadership may need only sermons and advisory help from interim pastors. Smaller churches often need more than just a visiting preacher and will benefit strongly from a temporary pastor with several responsibilities. Whatever the requirements, try to recommend the best person possible. Because the congregation's well-being is related to how quickly it's members can move into their new chapter, you should suggest only the best seminary professors, the most stimulating furloughed missionaries, or the most vibrant retired pastors. A healthy transition period requires a strong pulpit ministry.

Formation of a search committee. Representation on the search or pulpit committee is frequently specified in the church's constitution. But even if membership on the nominating committee, church board, or congregation at large is a requirement, it is critical that the right people be selected from the available name pool.

Most congregations try to ensure that their pulpit committee is *representative* of the church. Unfortunately, this practice may only safeguard long-established special interests. Nominating members who have shown sound judgment on other matters is better than trying to achieve a *fair* representation of male and female, young and old, and so on. A search committee with big picture team players is superior to a committee comprised of individuals selected to protect a particular interest group. Encouraging the church to draw together wise decision makers is part of the advisory role of a departing pastor.

Some churches wait until their former pastor has left before beginning their search process. Perhaps they feel it's rude to discuss a new mate while the old body's still warm. Maybe they anticipate a controlling pushiness on the part of their current minister. But the church that waits until the pastor has departed loses both valuable time and guidance. Perhaps the best counsel you can offer your church is *get moving*. Relieving the leadership's fears about your inordinate influence or hurt feelings will help them get on with the task of finding your replacement.

Call committee procedures. Myriad details cry out for attention during a pastor's last weeks in town, so it's not possible (or wise) to spend a great amount of time with the search committee. But most laypersons appreciate a cleric's counsel regarding call-committee procedures. You can guide them in setting realistic time frames. You can pass on forms and resources for soliciting information (see figs. 7–9 at the end of this chapter for samples). And you can get them in touch with adjudicatory leadership or a consultant experienced in the process.

Assessing the church's potential. Encouraging the leadership to undertake a congregational study and a community demographics survey is sound advice. Whether a church conducts its own survey or retains the services of a consulting firm, solid research is a prerequisite for planning. Congregational analyses measure the effectiveness of programs, giving patterns and congregational values. Community studies uncover data on growth rates, housing starts, economic status, age groupings, marital status, and types of local employment. The results of these comprehensive surveys enable the congregation to assess its needs, plan its future and guide the drafting of pastoral profile. They also help potential candidates measure fit with the church.

Orientation for the new minister. Advising church leaders on the benefits of an orientation committee can facilitate the transition of your successor.

First, this committee can compile biographical sketches of the congregants. For example, when my wife joined Calvary Church as children's minister, Barbara was delighted to be given a relatively new church family album. Each page in the large three-ring binder contained a picture of an individual or a family with descriptions of themselves. The album was a helpful tool for matching names and faces. It would be great if every church would give its new pastor such information.

Second, the committee can assist the pastoral family with housing. One church appointed a husband-and-wife team to ensure that the moving company placed furniture and boxes according to the pastor's sketched instructions. In another congregation, a volunteer crew refurbished the parsonage and manicured the surrounding grounds. These types of activities (and others, such as a pantry shower) do not happen without planning and supervision, yet they provide a warm welcome to the pastoral family in their new home.

Third, an orientation committee can make themselves available to the pastoral family upon their arrival. A list of doctors, department stores, banks, supermarkets, and service centers is useful, of course, but helping the clergy family register children for school, license their vehicles, or turn on utilities is an even deeper gesture of hospitality.

Fourth, an orientation committee can pass on a welcome letter from you, the departing pastor, to your successor. (A copy of the letter can be offered to the chairperson of the orientation committee to alleviate any suspicions.) This communiqué should provide positive background information about the membership and community. Your task is not to make procedural suggestions but to present a realistic picture of the church and thereby save hours of time for the new minister. For example, seasonal traditions, community events and neighborhood activities that have had historical significance are worth delineating. Most new pastors would also appreciate a list of people with special needs and the names of church prospects. A letter of greeting and orientation can provide a personal word from you, someone who has *been there*. Encouraging the formation of an orientation committee is a gracious gift to your pastoral replacement.

A Gracious and Final Release

A good indicator of a pastor's spiritual maturity is the graciousness of his or her exit. A hireling hits the road focused only on the next job and paycheck, but a shepherd departs with a show of concern for the flock's well-being. Your demeanor during the last days of transition will reveal much about your character.

A gracious and final release includes the following things.

A farewell message. The old saying is true: "We know not what the future holds, but we know who holds the future." While expressing personal feelings is natural and appropriate, a pastor's last public address should be a message of hope that reminds the congregation of God's goodness, faithfulness, and wisdom. One pastor used Philippians 1:9–11 for a sermon that he called "A Personal Prayer." Another pastor focused on the farewell messages of Paul, titling the sermon "Finally, Friends." Another pastor gave "A Call to Unity" from 1 Corinthians 1:4–17. Several colleagues shared the meaningfulness of exalting Christ around a final communion celebration.

A reception. Healthy closure is facilitated if a reception is held on the pastor's last Sunday at the church. Formats range from a simple receiving line to a gala dinner with cordial *roast* or other appropriate program. Sometimes, especially following forced termination, the last place a pastor wants to be is shaking the hands of smiling people who are saying, "Best wishes." Nevertheless, many parishioners will want to express their sincere appreciation for your ministry. You deny them that opportunity if your preoccupation with malcontents disallows a formal good-bye. You also miss an opportunity for forgiveness and growth (let alone modeling such) if you refuse to participate in a final celebration of the pastor/people relationship. A receiving line is almost always a pastor's last personal contact with most of individuals in the congregation. A simple *thank you*, handshake, hug, or smile can express as much warmth for a person as a whole year's worth of sermons. While not allowing specific individuals to dominate the conversation, you should relax and expect these good-byes to take some time.

A note of appreciation. The last communication to the flock should be a note of thanks. Expressing appreciation for any parting gifts is appropriate, of course, but it is more important to show your gratitude for the opportunity you've had to serve the congregation. One pastor believes that "a final word to your congregation in which you acknowledge your actions and feelings not only will help you maintain your integrity and reputation, but can be healing for the congregation that must now grieve its loss of you. Gratitude expressed to them for their ministry to you as well as for the opportunity to minister to them should be a part of this confessional and intimate moment."[3]

Praying for the congregation and its new pastor. Upholding the church in prayer is natural for a minister who is concerned with the well-being of the flock. Praying for the congregation affects both the members and their departing pastor. Intercession regarding the faithfulness of volunteers, selection of a new pastor, receptivity to the new cleric, stability and growth, and glorification of God is an outflow of love that will be long remembered.

Discouraging dependence upon you. After years of closeness, of bonding between pastor and people, sometimes it's hard to let go, yet a gracious and final release discourages continued contact with former congregants. Letters, phone calls, or personal visits to them will slow down *grief work,* foster disunity, and undermine the new pastoral leadership. Better to receive information on the congregation from the church newsletter, communication with the new pastor, or notes on Christmas cards than to keep resurfacing.

Exceptions to this practice may be a few calls during the interim period or the first year away (perhaps most needed by family members). If vacation or business plans take you back to the area, you should avoid making personal stops from home to home. Although you might accept an invitation from a family wanting to host a dessert open house, encouraging the current pastor to attend would be wise.

Summary

Each of us proceeds through seasons of change. We drive through different neighborhoods in our journey of life. Congregations likewise move through several passages of change. Grief joins our journey at transition points; we feel loss, the price of separation. But because hope also meets us at these intersections, we should feel energized and newly challenged. As a shepherd of Christ's flock, your final work at a church is to accompany people on their journey from grief to hope. Although the trip takes longer for some people than for others, a gracious release enables both you and your former church to move ahead with joyful anticipation.

Figure 7

Pastoral Search Committee
Task Chart and Timetable

Task	Completion Date	Responsibility
Periodic communication with congregation (every 3 weeks)		
Worship folder and newsletter announcements to church office		
Evaluate church questionnaires		
Develop prospectus:		
Annual report		
Church constitution and by-laws		
Staff job descriptions		
Community profile		
Pastoral profile		
Church profile and personality		
Obtain names of potential candidates		
Send letter to potential candidates		
Send follow-up letters		
Review of candidates with denominational advisors		
Begin reference and background check		
Develop committee members' questionnaire		
Start visitation process		
Determine candidating program		
Invitation letter to prospective candidate		
Arrange details for candidate's visit to the church		
Prepare candidate's contract for church approval		
Welcome God's man to the church[1]		

---

1. From Dennis Newton Baker, "A Pastoral Search Manual for Conservative Baptist Association of Southern California" (unpublished Doctor of Ministries dissertation, 1992, Talbot School of Theology). Used by permission.

Figure 8

Sample Senior Pastor Recommendation

Instructions: To assist your Pulpit Committee in considering candidates, please complete all portions of this form.[1] If information is unavailable, please indicate "NA" in that section. Completed forms should be submitted to the church office or to a member of the Pulpit Committee.

Recommendation made by:_____

Candidate's name:_____

Current information:

    Title:_____

    Mailing address:

        (Street)_____

        (City)_____

        (State & Zip Code)_____

    Telephone number:_____

    How long in current position?_____

    How long in ministry?_____

    Educational background:_____

_____

_____

_____

Please state your personal knowledge of the individual (i.e., former pastor, have heard him preach, name suggested to you by friend or relative, etc.).

---

1. From Colony Park Church, Edina, Minnesota. Used by permission.

Please state the specific reasons and/or qualifications that have caused you to recommend this individual.

Please supply the name, address, and phone number of individuals we could contact to provide further information and references for this individual.

Figure 9

Ministry Survey

Trinity's leadership teams invite your input as we seek God's guidance to face the challenges of the new century.[1] Thank you for your participation.

1. How long have you been attending Trinity Church? _____

2. How long have you been a member? _____

3. Please describe your Sunday A.M. attendance level at Trinity:
   ___ Regular attendee (3–4 times per month)
   ___ Occasional attendee (1–2 times per month)
   ___ Other (please describe)

4. Please describe your involvement level at Trinity Church beyond Sunday attendance:
   ___ Very involved   ___ Somewhat involved
   ___ Only A.M. services   ___ Other

5. In what year were you born? _____

6. What is your gender:
   ___ Male   ___ Female

7. What is your marital status:
   ___ Single   ___ Married   ___ Widowed

8. In your opinion, what are Trinity's major areas of strength?

---

1. Used by permission of Trinity Church, Mesa, Arizona.

9. There are many ways to strengthen a church's ministry. In what areas do you think Trinity should improve? What would you suggest?

10. Are there any concerns or unresolved issues that Trinity should address?

    ___ No   ___ Yes (if "yes," please describe)

11. Describe the senior pastor that Trinity needs for effective ministry in 2012.

16

JUMPING OUT OF
THE BLOCKS

Many track races are won because of a superior start. Runners who are slow out of the blocks struggle to catch up with the field. Those who get an early lead have a better chance of victory. A good race requires a fast start, a consistent run, and an energetic kick to the finish line.

The previous chapter emphasized the importance of a strong finish. Preparing a congregation for transition requires running hard through your final day with them. However, even as you complete that last leg of the race, you should begin formulating the strategy for your next challenge. By building momentum before arrival, keeping family adjustments a priority, and practicing some strategic do's and don'ts, you can get up to speed quickly in your new ministry.

Building Momentum Prior to Arrival

Making a good start with a new congregation requires gathering key information and planning your strategy before arriving. Specific preparatory actions can facilitate a smooth beginning. These momentum-building activities include the following.

Compiling family-oriented information. Shortly after accepting a pastoral call, ask the congregation to compile information that will ease the transition for your family. One colleague suggests asking the call committee to involve the entire church in the process: "There's something you could send us that we believe is fairly important . . . ask members of the congregation to share favorite places or pieces of helpful information. Give everyone a piece of paper after church and have them write one or two things they would want to know if they were new in town."[1] Information about grocery stores, discount outlets, recreational centers, favorite restaurants and other tidbits from the membership may reveal much about both the community and the congregation.

Finalizing living arrangements. Determining where you will live is fundamental to any move. Decisions regarding housing are best made early and documented in the letter of call. For example, one pastor stipulated that repainting of the parsonage (choice of colors by the clergy family) be done before his arrival. During the candidating weekend, another minister and his wife selected the neighborhood in which they wanted to live and asked a member of the congregation to do some prescreening of homes according to certain criteria. After looking at pictures and descriptions, the minister's spouse traveled back to the new community to close on a final selection. Another pastor asked a clergy friend to secure a lease on a rental home within a specified school district. Since he and his wife wanted their children to go to the school attended by most of the other children in the congregation, they knew the neighborhood in which they would need to reside.

Although housing markets vary greatly across the country, and purchasing power in a new community can price a minister away from the average house in a church, pastors who purchase their own homes find it less problematic if they select a neighborhood typical of most members. Buying at the extremes of the housing continuum can cause embarrassment or resentment within the congregation. The potential for ministry, not a new residence, is the reason for moving, yet solidifying appropriate living arrangements facilitates the transition.

Determining initial preaching directions. The last thing a congregation may need from its new pastor is another series on Ephesians! Knowing about the preaching and teaching content of your predecessor helps avoid this problem. One pastor, shortly after accepting a call, asked the church secretary to mail him a list of the former pastor's sermon titles and texts for the last two years. Another pastor asked to borrow bulletins from the previous year, thus gaining insight into both messages and the nature of worship. Another colleague suggests trying to get a videotape of a morning service or at least one of the former pastor's sermons.

Once you enter the new community, you will be bombarded with a host of family and church demands. Thus, it's profitable before arrival to plan two months of messages to share with the new flock. Choose your themes on the basis of what you already know about the congregation and from other information acquired during the transition period. One minister, for example, began his new pastorate with messages on the Holy Spirit and the importance of the Spirit-filled life. Another pastor offered a miniseries on *The Church Body* based on Romans 12 and 1 Corinthians 12. A third pastor presented three sermons on the reliability and authority of the Bible, pointing to the source from which all subsequent messages derive their validity. Pastors who begin preparing their first few sermons before they arrive at their new church will find it easier to cope with the initial pressures and to build momentum for their ministry.

Organizing a collection of transferable materials. Just as reinventing the wheel is a waste of time, adapting existing resources to a new situation beats recreating them. Go through your files! By assembling a set of materials for first-time-visitor letters, seasonal letters, sermon notes, ministry descriptions, and seminar handouts, a new pastor can reduce start-up time. By photocopying personal notes sent to celebrate graduations, weddings, birthdays or to ease bereavement or illness, avoids having to struggle to find just the right word to say. Newsletter articles are also worth saving, since a given article may be appropriate on another occasion. Even registration cards and other forms may prove useful. Committees at the new church may also benefit from examining procedure manuals from your former congregation.

Many of the resources we pastors compile will be appropriate for only a memories file. Even usable material will likely need adaptation.

Nevertheless, organizing a collection of good resources from your former church and other good congregations can save time in the new church.

Making Family Adjustment a Priority

Pastors asked to identify their greatest concern about making a move often reply, "Helping my family, especially my spouse, feel comfortable in our new situation." You will probably discover, as have many of our colleagues, that your own adjustment during a pastoral transition is relatively easy in contrast to that of your loved ones. Even as you enter a changed environment for your ministry, your routine and activities remain basically the same as they were in your former church. You will still be expected to preach and teach, lead and manage, and counsel and care. Your calendar will be crowded with the same types of meetings and appointments as before.

Adjustment for your children, however, will be more difficult. Yes, they will study the same subjects at school, but in their old environment they were also busy with extracurricular activities. Now they will have free time on their hands and no friends with whom to enjoy it.

Harder still is the adjustment for spouses. In the former community, they probably had a career or an established routine of volunteer work, but now they're unemployed. Then they had a support network of friends, but now they don't know anyone. They had an identity of their own in their previous situation, but now they're only known as *the pastor's spouse.*

Although jumping out of the blocks at a new church does require thrusting yourself into parish activities as soon as possible, any start that ignores the needs of your family is a false start. Your enthusiasm might look good to the crowd, but it won't last long if your family is unhappy in their new environment. You can make the transition easier for your loved ones by doing the following:

Accept their feelings of loss. Even when family members believe that the Lord is guiding a change and are eager about the relocation, they will still feel the grief of separation. Now is not the time to tell your family, "Get with the program!" Availing yourself to them as a friend who understands and accepts their waves of emotion is far more helpful.

Recognizing and dealing sensibly with the normal reactions to loss is important. One writer shares the following illustration:

> In the weeks immediately before and after a move, tempers can get especially short. We allow each other some space for anger and loneliness. One spring as we prepared to move, my husband said, 'You seem to be mad at me lately. Is there something wrong?'
>
> 'Of course not!' I answered, rather too quickly. When I gave it some thought, however, I realized I was angry. I didn't want to leave my job, friends, and neighbors, or the sugar maples and lilac bushes I had come to love. It didn't matter that the decision to move had been made prayerfully by both of us; I still felt angry.
>
> That helped me understand how our children feel, helping me give our daughters freedom to express their emotions. We try to express anger in positive ways and not at one another.[2]

Keep farewells upbeat. Because celebrative closures make everyone feel better, quietly leaving neighborhood and friends without a backward glance is a mistake. A good *good-bye* includes reliving special times together as a couple. Visiting sentimental places or dining at a favorite restaurant will preserve good memories. Going to dinner with friends, or having a party before you leave are equally important.

Farewell bashes for our children are likewise appropriate. One writer suggests,

> Parents can supply cookies and punch for a good-bye party if the child's school doesn't take this kind of initiative. Most teachers would be happy to include this in the school day shortly before the move takes place.[3]

Another person shares this experience:

> Our daughters were only six and eight years old when we
> moved from our home in Iowa. We planned one last party
> for their friends—the ultimate slumber party. Seventeen
> girls spent the night: eight-year-olds in the basement, six-
> year-olds upstairs. They partied and played, ate dozens of
> hotdogs from a makeshift table of sawhorses and two-by-
> fours in the driveway. The next morning they hugged one
> another and said good-bye.[4]

Another experienced traveler offered this suggestion:

> Before leaving town, buy your child an address book and
> let him collect addresses and phone numbers of his friends.
> Allow him to exchange photos as well. He can make his
> own "change of address" cards—decorated with colorful
> stickers.[5]

Make plans for reconnecting. Farewells are easier to handle if you can
expect to see special friends again. The finality of separation is minimized by making plans to reconnect. Several colleagues suggest scheduling a vacation trip back to the old community or inviting your
children's friends to your new home. One pastor shared how his family rendezvoused with former neighbors at a midpoint location during the summer after the move. One clergy family attended family
camp where members of the old church were in attendance. Another
family joined friends at a week-long couples conference. Making plans
for reconnecting doesn't eliminate grief, but it does give everyone
something pleasant to anticipate. It provides hope, and hope invariably softens the feelings of loss.

Obtain records. Obtaining important documents before leaving further facilitates a family's adjustment to a new community. For example, families with children will need to secure pertinent school
information, including transcripts of student progress, results of stan-
dardized testing, and a list of recent textbooks. Letters of progress

from the former school can detail classroom performance and explain the conditions in which your children are most productive.

It is also important to obtain medical and dental records for the whole family. Schools will require immunization histories, and doctors will want to know of previous procedures. Either plan to bring those with you, or have them transferred as soon as you select the professionals who will oversee your health.

Before leaving your old community, be sure that you have a valid birth certificate for every family member. In many situations, only an original birth certificate (with an official seal) is acceptable for proof of age or citizenship. Taking time to acquire these documents before they are actually needed is easier than trying to rush them through the processing at a later date.

Spend extra time with your children. Pastors who are highly energized by the challenge of a new church often let their work squeeze out family time. Yet, during relocation, parents are usually the only *friends* their children have. By giving extra attention to your children, you help them feel that they are more important to you than the job that uprooted them.

Fun family time can begin with the relocation itself. Colleagues share the following advice.

- Travel for relatively short periods of time, staying at child-friendly motels.
- Allow children to stay up later than usual (as a special treat, let the little ones bounce on the beds).
- Visit famous sights along the journey.
- Travel in two cars equipped with CB radios or cellular phones.
- Stop at the homes of family and friends along the way.
- Allow children to choose meals while traveling.
- Collect postcards from different states, some to keep and others to send back to friends.

Once you arrive in the new community, deepen family friendships by exploring the community together. Make time for activities such as building models; visiting a museum; playing catch, miniature golf, or computer games; driving to the shore; racing go-carts; water-skiing; or tenting overnight in the backyard. Such events will strengthen any family relationship and thereby help everyone feel more comfortable in the new environment.

In addition to personal time with your children, encourage their participation in peer activities. Registering them for a library reading hour, signing up for soccer, or joining a local scouting group might take some gentle nudging. Yet, in the long run, they will profit through this easing into the community.

As a pastor, you will always have people who want to see you and meetings that need to be scheduled. You won't, however, always have children at home. Soon, they might not even notice whether you're around! It's *now* when your presence is critical.

Ease your spouse's transition. Ministers who reflect on their first few months in a new church suggest two primary ways to help a partner deal with the loneliness of relocation. First, they stress the importance of spending personal time together. Second, they note the value of involvement in the community.

One couple spent quality one-on-one time as they worked on their new house. "It gave us, my wife especially, something to invest ourselves in." Another couple made it a point to have a lunch date once a week, although normally they ate out only once a month. A third couple commented, "Much of our relational processing happened on early morning walks together." Experiencing meaningful shared moments as a couple provides stability and companionship in unfamiliar territory.

Participation in local activities, either alone or as a couple, further facilitates a partner's adjustment. One pastor said, "It's helpful to respond to people's invitations to go out; it gets you and your spouse familiar with new people and your new surroundings." Another minister admitted, "Personally, I really didn't want to join the couples' study group because I already had enough church-related meetings and evenings out. But I knew our participation was important to my wife, so we began attending." Another colleague shared this experience: "During our first year, my wife took a course in accounting at the local college. It was only an introductory course, and she already had some business experience. But it was an enjoyable experience for her, and it was good for her just to get out. She also became involved in several community projects and started attending Bible Study Fellowship." Every community offers opportunities for personal enrichment. Involvement in these activities will make the transitional experience more pleasant for the entire family.

Strategic Start-up *Do's* and *Don'ts*

What advice would you give colleagues moving to a new church? Asking this question of pastors and ministerial groups around the country generated some helpful guidelines for the start–up period. Practices worth embracing, and to avoid, comprise the following list.

Strategic Do's

Do develop vision. Without vision, a pastor merely parishes. If you paint a picture of what the church can become, the congregation will live up to that image. Sermon illustrations, newsletters, and personal conversations are all useful in communicating vision.

Do be realistic in expectations. Some things will take longer than planned. Some people will not like you. Interruptions will occur. Surprises will happen. Reality requires some flexibility.

Do build relationships. People don't care how much you know until they know how much you care. This is especially true in a small church.

Do work hard. Becoming a slave to work is a sickness (workaholism), yet enjoying a full day's work reaps benefits and builds enthusiasm.

Do maintain regular office hours. Ministry requires flexible hours, yet people should know when they can reach you. If we are available in afternoons but not in the mornings, that's understandable. But when we are seldom available, we're open to criticism.

Do schedule family time. Unless you block out family time on your calendar (even months ahead of time), the demands of the church will fill your schedule.

Do protect your spouse from unrealistic congregational expectations. Most churches no longer hold to the *two-for-one* philosophy, whereby a minister and spouse are hired for one salary. Yet, most churches will expect some involvement on the part of the spouse. Your assistance will be needed to ensure reasonable balance.

Do focus members on achievable tasks. Because positive feelings are built in a congregation with every small victory, it's important that plans and activities are achievable.

Do celebrate successes. Accomplishments are highly motivational: *success breeds success.* Informing people about the good happenings also weakens critics' arguments.

Do attend social gatherings when possible. Attending adult socials, home study groups, parents' meetings, preschool Christmas programs, etc., brings you in contact with most large clusters of the congregation at a small expenditure of time.

Do schedule open houses. "Although I cannot get into every one of your homes, I will invite each of you into *our* home," announced one pastor. By using existing classes or small groups, or by subdividing a congregation alphabetically, over time you can cycle the entire membership through your home.

Do establish a disciplined pattern of study. Study time that is not blocked into your schedule will disappear. Building a routine of study and communicating its importance to the congregation establishes the practice as an important priority.

Do develop an exercise routine. Stamina, mental outlook, and even the ability to handle emotional stress are directly related to one's physical conditioning. Maintaining a three-day-a-week routine of stretching, muscle strengthening, and aerobic workout is beneficial.

Do adjust leadership styles. Self-starters merely need a leader's go-ahead whereas followers require more focused direction. Varying your natural leadership style (though not altering it radically) brings the best results.

Do implement change carefully. With the coming of new leadership, people expect some change. In fact, the larger the church, the more its members expect innovations. But moving too quickly will increase resistance. Ensuring that a specific change is the best alternative and then communicating that change early and thoroughly helps people adjust.

Do retain present leadership. Some members of the board or staff may need to be negotiated out of leadership, but initially you do not want the problems that this action brings. "I don't know of a terminated staff member who didn't leave behind a trail of bitter friends," reflects one pastor.

Do practice MBWA: Ministry by Walking Around. This keeps you engaged with the flock. Therefore, get out of the office and spend time with people in *their* environments.

Do participate in local ministerial fellowships. It's tough for a single log to keep aflame, but a pile of wood burns strongly. Colleagues provide mutual support, ministry insights, and a broader overview of Christendom.

Do maintain a sense of humor. Intensity without release can kill. Healthful, appropriate humor (never sarcasm) lightens your spirit, makes you attractive to others, and can diffuse tense situations.

Strategic Don'ts

Don't assume that the way things were done in your former church will work now. Local variables influence ministry effectiveness. Programs that have flourished in one location have failed in another location. Contextual sensitivity is critical to your success.

Don't criticize a predecessor. Along with weaknesses and failures, everyone has areas of strength and success. Even a minister who was asked to resign leaves behind many people who were personally touched and appreciative. You cannot elevate yourself by trying to bring down another person.

Don't kill off "endangered species." Allow ineffective programs to die by themselves. Simply begin quality programs that address needs.

Don't be a revolutionary. Many congregations have struggled with innovations initiated by a pastor with startling new ideas. People have called you to lead but not to drive them into exhaustion (or confusion).

Don't merely recycle former sermons. It's easy, under the pressures of startup, to avoid hours of preparation by using previous sermons. Such efficiency is commendable but only when a message is appropriate for congregational needs. Try a fresh approach that is sensitive to the voice of the Spirit and relevant to your new people.

Don't send 'you' messages. Using *we* and *our,* especially in your preaching, implies that you are one with the congregation. *You* messages stamp you as standoffish or above your audience.

Don't keep hidden agendas. Business executives recognize the benefit of a *no-surprises* approach in company operations. Revealing all of your dreams at once is not necessary, but manipulating people or situations for undisclosed purposes fosters resentment.

Don't expect everyone to like you. Most pastors know that they can't please everyone, but they still struggle when someone leaves the church because he or she is *not being fed*. Tougher still is the situation when antagonists remain in the congregation. Over time, even they may warm to you, especially if you minister to them in crises. Others might never like you, but that's part of leadership.

Don't play favorites. The nature of ministry requires investing yourself more in some people than in others. (Lay leaders probably need the greatest amount of our time.) But while you spend a disproportionate amount of time with some people, all of the members of the flock must feel that you are concerned with their well-being.

Don't engage in power struggles. In an *I win; you lose* confrontation, *everyone loses*. Few battles are worth jeopardizing the outcome of the war. Much more is accomplished by identifying the people with authority in the church and making them your allies.

Don't respond when angry. Frequently, our *reactions* get us into more trouble than our actions. You might not avoid being misunderstood or criticized, but you can guard against immature knee-jerk reactions that diminish your credibility.

Don't gossip or share information indiscreetly. Talking negatively about one individual to another is not wise. The third party will be angry or hurt when word eventually gets back to him or her. (And it will!) Furthermore, the person with whom you are sharing might think, *If he criticizes Mary in her absence, what will he say about* me *when I'm not here?*

Don't be afraid to apologize. Pastors do not become infallible upon ordination. (You can probably think of things that you've said in previous ministries that you would like to retract.) Admitting a misunderstanding or failure strengthens character and sets an example that others may follow.

Don't accept leadership on denominational or local committees during the first year. Participation in ministerial associations and community task forces is important, but accepting responsibilities in such organizations in the first year is not wise. Before offering leadership to the larger church, use your time and energy adjusting to your new congregation.

Don't get discouraged. Focusing on the negative is unhealthy. Even during trying times, remember that seeds are being sown, lives are being touched, and a future is being shaped.

Summary

Summer Olympic highlights often center on track and field, and few events are more electrifying than the sprints. Many times during these games, we have seen races won or lost at the start of an event.

For a transitional pastor, the most critical game with a new congregation is the long-distance run, but here, too, a good start is essential for running a good race. Building momentum before arrival, making family adjustments a priority, and practicing strategic start-up dos and don'ts gets you out of the blocks smoothly. After that, if you pace your strides wisely and listen to the Coach's sideline directions, you'll hear cheers for your victory at the finish line.

17

RETIRING OR REPOSITIONING?

Retirement! HOW DOES THAT WORD HIT YOU? Some people look forward to this life stage with eagerness. After many seasons of hard work, taking greater control of one's schedule looks appealing. Other people, however, resent this approaching life stage. For them, it feels as though someone is replacing them and that they are no longer needed.

The thought of retirement is scary for many people because this transition is unexperienced and unknown. When we move from one ministry assignment to another, we have a pretty good idea of what we are getting into. People and activities may change, but our role remains the same. But as we look toward retirement, we must make choices of residence. Questions of finance and security become critical. Most significant are issues related to identity. In the words of one colleague, "To the person who has invested twenty or thirty years in a meaningful career, . . . that career has become an extension of himself. It has brought a sense of worth and dignity, and has therefore been a major source of building esteem."[1] Since some people's identity is so wrapped up in what they do, their transition into retirement can rock the very foundation of their being.

Retirement is a phenomenon of culture. Affluence has made it particularly possible in the Western world. But the expression *working for a living* should not be associated with only financial well-being. Work is important to our overall well-being.

God Himself instituted work. Healthful productivity was God's design for humanity since Creation. Unfortunately, with *the Fall* work also became toilsome. But this labor associated with work should not mislead people to think that work itself is bad or should be avoided. God Himself works. And those who are created in His image likewise find fulfillment in profitable work. One colleague illustrates the point:

> [As retirees,] . . . we will still want to feel needed, worthwhile, and productive. We will still need, too, to feel that we're growing, that we're useful, and that our existence is important. This is why so many retirees, after spending a few vacation months on the golf course, come to miss—if not indeed to long for—the shattering sound of the alarm clock waking them up to the involvement and challenge of the world of work. Putter in hand, they come to the startling realization that on the day they retire, they walked away from a large part of themselves.[2]

The reason many people today struggle with later maturity is that they have an unbiblical understanding of retirement. This statement should not be misunderstood to mean that we cannot bring to conclusion remunerated service. But it does affirm that to be fully human, we must remain productive. As one writer has noted, "Work supplies an answer to some of the deepest and most basic of all human drives; the need to produce something, the need to create something, the need satisfy curiosity, the need to be useful, the need to be needed."[3]

Therefore, retirement is best viewed not as an ending so much as a beginning. We are not retiring *from* something but *to* something. We are not retreating; we are repositioning.

Many opportunities lie before a gifted minister. Upon retirement, some pastors have become chaplains, consultants, fundraisers, authors, and interim pastors. One minister stated, "If you are in a city, there are a lot of churches around that are looking for part-time people." Another friend who has been serving for seven years in such a capacity reflected, "When I left my full-time position, I cleared out my desk and said out loud, 'Lord, is this all there is?' I soon found out the answer to that question was a resounding 'no.'" Presently, he and his wife are experiencing some of the most fulfilling ministry of their lives, and within parameters that they have chosen.

Letting Go

One of the questions that I asked of pastors who have moved into the repositioning stage was, "How did you know when it was time finally to resign?" Some of those who responded thought that their church was at a critical stage, and they had to decide if they could stay long enough to see it through the next season of ministry. One minister expressed it thus: "I felt I had to make some long range plans and thought it was best for the church to get someone new who could bring into realization their vision. Their next chapter would likely have the best outcome with new leadership."

Some of the pastors interviewed indicated that their movement into this stage was forced upon them. Some of them even felt pressured to retire a couple of years sooner than they personally desired. In the words of one friend, "I really wanted to hang in there until I was sixty-five, but we were in decline, and I didn't have the ideas or energy to remedy the situation. However, even at that, I probably wouldn't have gotten out of the nest without a few of the church leaders pushing me a bit."

A number of other ministers indicated that their movement into this life stage was determined years earlier. They had calculated the impact of their retirement on themselves and on their churches, and moved toward a positive transition. One minister even brought onto the staff an associate who became the senior pastor two years later.

One colleague described how a group of five men surrounded him for about eight months. He said, "They helped me formulate when I should leave, how it should happen, and the celebration that would bring closure to this chapter for the church and me." Moving into the retirement stage intentionally, rather than reactively, gives both our church and ourselves a fresh start for that which lies beyond.

Another pastor used an analogy to explain this particular transition: "I see pastoral ministry like a relay race. Each pastor takes the baton from a predecessor, runs a great lap, and then hands it off to a successor. In my last church, I ran a good race, then handed off the baton to a new shepherd. My only responsibility now was to get off the track." Although this might sound easy, everyone who was interviewed agreed that the letting go was not easy. Consider the words of one pastor: "Although I wanted to throw off all the work my job involved, I didn't want to give up the keys to my office. This familiar place comforted me. . . . My office was like a secure space ship saving me from drifting meaninglessly into the great void of retirement."[4]

Another minister who took retirement after twenty-five years of service in his last congregation describes his experience thus: "I felt like I was a man without a country; a man without a church. I no longer had a group of people looking to me. I still carried the burden of the church for years. It was especially hard for my wife and me when things weren't going well, but I was no longer in a position to do anything about it."

For the long-term well-being of the congregation, and for our own emotional health, we need to move on. Affirming this view, one pastor stated, "I didn't take phone calls; I absented myself from the church for a year; and I avoided triangulation." Although this clergy couple still has friends in the congregation, they understand boundaries and support the new leadership.

Another colleague related how some of the board members wanted to give him the status of "pastor emeritus." He turned the offer down because he thought the church needed to be future oriented rather than past oriented. "It was important that I leave," he said, "therefore, I wasn't available for weddings or funerals or counseling."

So how do you let go? The words of this pastor succinctly summarized it: *"Just stay out of it!"* Although that is easier said than done, the blessings of the repositioning life stage can happen only when we bring closure and accept the finality of the past.

Stages of Later Adulthood

Most of the pastors with whom I have talked move into the retirement stage between the ages of sixty-two and sixty-eight. A few wish they could have transitioned sooner, but they were not able financially. Others wish they could have remained a bit longer, but they either didn't have the energy or the encouragement to do so. Once into the transition, however, all of them seemed content with life in this new chapter.

To best understand this new season, rather than talking about retirement, it is more helpful to talk about the stages of retirement, or stages of maturity. Gerontologists divide later adulthood into early maturity, middle maturity, and later maturity. Speaking on the lighter side, one colleague referred to these stages as *Go-Go, Slow-Go, and No-Go.* While each person's biological clock will differ, these stages reflect the ages of sixty-two to seventy-five, seventy-two to eighty-five, and eighty-five plus. Obviously, energy levels and opportunities for physical activity and travel are greater in early maturity. But regardless of the stage, we should maximize our capacity for growth.

The Bible relates that the child Jesus "increased in wisdom and stature, and in favor with God and man" (Luke 2:52 KJV). In a certain sense, this maturation process never ceases. Throughout all of our years, we can keep learning. If reading becomes difficult, we can use audio books. Flexibility, strength, and aerobic exercise, even in modest proportions, will let us feel better and help us get around more easily. Practicing the spiritual disciplines that work best for us keeps us centered on the One who is preeminent. In maintaining friendships (whether traveling together in our sixties or talking on the telephone in our eighties), we are enriched through Christian community. Healthy people stretch their minds, keep active physically, stay close to the heart of God, and nurture personal relationships.

One advisor summarizes it:

> Retirement is not the cessation of productivity and worth. On the contrary, your retirement can represent a giant step of tremendous growth and progress. The key to making this

a reality is your taking steps—right now!—to make sure that, when retirement comes, you are retiring to something. Something you feel is more worthwhile, yes. Something you enjoy more, yes. Something more of your own choosing, yes. But, most importantly, something that stretches you, keeps you involved in life . . . and keeps you "growing."[5]

So whether one is traveling with a construction team to Mexico, serving as a volunteer chaplain in a small retirement home, or hosting a community Bible study, remaining active in kingdom service will keep us focused on the race and the prize ahead.

Sage Points

Books and articles abound regarding later adulthood and no doubt will increase with baby boomers aging. Much of that information applies to people in all walks of life, so take advantage of the insights of those who have gone before us. In addition, however, let's benefit from the discoveries of career ministers who have made this transition. Their counsel is consolidated into the following eight bits of advice.

Plan early. We hear the following expressions all the time: "Where has this past year gone? I can't believe how time is flying!" Life seems to move quickly, especially for those who are fully engaged in meaningful service. Boomers who feel as though they just got out of college can't believe their retirement is just around the corner.

A few of the colleagues with whom I talk left their full-time positions simply trusting God for future direction. Most, however, began charting their future course during the ending phase of their last pastorate. There is value in repositioning (moving into something else) while we are still in a present ministry.

Perhaps you'd like to serve as a traveling chaplain in RV communities or national parks. If so, look at the options and begin networking now. If you'd like to consider a part-time staff position, what would it look like, and where are they available? Again, start working your networks.

Perhaps you'd like to begin your own ministry. One friend suggests, "If you are interested in developing a small business to augment your income, get it started well before retirement. Many small businesses fail during the first two years. Should your first attempt follow this path, you have time to try some others. If you wait until you are retired, you may panic and continue to row a sinking boat. Talk to people who own small businesses to get some idea as to what it is all about. The key question is, "For what goods or services are people looking that I am capable of producing and that I can do with simplicity?"

One colleague considered transforming a hobby into a small business, but he concluded, "Although we thought we could enjoy running an antique shop, we loved our work with people over the years and thought we'd be more productive continuing with people than opening the shop." This type of assessment is best made while still in one's present ministry.

Team it! The repositioning of later adulthood doesn't happen for just the pastor but also his spouse. Therefore, decisions in this season dare not be made with only the clergy's desire and giftedness in mind. One pastor affirmed, "We need to be on the same page with our spouse. The issue of retirement is not only what are my strengths and desires, but also what are her strengths, and what does she want to do."

Earlier in a clergy marriage the employment of the primary breadwinner heavily influenced vocational decisions and lifestyle arrangements. As we reevaluate opportunities in later adulthood, however, a new flexibility can allow us to work toward deeper consensus. And if an impasse should arise, now is the opportunity for the clergy's spouse to break the tie.

Financial restructuring. As we reach our mid-sixties, opportunities before us will be screened through a number of grids. One critical grid is that of finances. When asked, "What advice would you give to pastors moving into the stages of retirement?" one friend, a financial advisor, responded,

- Make every effort to have your house paid prior to retirement. If this is not possible, make major additional payments to principle for several years prior to retirement.

- Commit to be totally free of credit card debt at retirement time, and then only use cards for convenience, when you know you have the funds to pay off the entire balance each month.
- Plan your car acquisitions such that you go into retirement with a car that will last you for several years.
- Consider the real need to relocate to a part of the country where the cost of housing, utilities, and necessities are lower than where you live now.
- If you have significant assets, engage a financial planner to help you prepare for restructuring, and get educated in the process.
- Community colleges offer courses for people to help plan for retirement. Take advantage of them.[6]

Capitalize on Strengths. After thirty or forty years of ministry, you would think that upon retirement most of our colleagues would want to do something completely different. However, what I have discovered is that the gift mix that makes people effective in ministry is usually the same gift mix to which they will turn to in part-time or volunteer service. When we add to that gift mix other talents and assets that we've acquired, and then consider the needs around us, a directional template for service can emerge.

For example, several of the repositioned ministers whom I interviewed incorporated their own ministries. One asset that pastors might overlook is all of the people with whom they have developed friendships over the years and who shared a passion for a particular type of ministry. For example, one pastor was concerned with racial reconciliation, another with assisting young parents, and a third with missions in Mexico. In each of these situations, former ministry friends gave significant volunteer service and financial support to these ventures.

Find a good church home. Retired clergy tend to reside either where their children live or where they consider *home*. Home might be where they grew up or where they spent a significant part of their ministry service. Some clergy will remain in the community of their last congregation.

The challenge when remaining in the same church is the temptation toward overinvolvement, to be drawn into leadership issues. We have already discussed the importance of letting go, so we can understand the pastor who advised, "In these situations, we need to have a hands-off attitude!"

The challenge when joining another church (as a lay person now) is coping with feelings of insignificance. Before, we were at the center of all action; now we are on the outside of everything. Before, we knew everything that was happening in people's lives; now we're strangers to most folks. Before, we determined schedules and events; now no one asks our opinion.

Although most of our colleagues initially struggled to get past these feelings, they eventually discovered the freedom of simply living in community. Before, these pastors felt the pressure of planning worship services for people with vastly different preferences; now they are simply lovers of God. Before, they worried about assimilation and people falling through the cracks; now they can befriend just a few people. Before, they felt the pressures of staffing volunteer services; now they are just personal servants of Christ.

As we conclude the season of full-time professional ministry, it will be time to practice what we've preached for decades: all believers need to live in community. We, too, need to know and be known. We will need an environment in which we can learn, worship, and serve. Colleagues who have gone before us warn that the change from authority and position can be difficult, but it is also enjoyable and rewarding.

Simplify your lifestyle. In Sunday school we used to sing, "This world is not my home; I'm just a passing through." But for just passing through it sure seems like we've collected a lot of stuff on the journey. So one colleague advised, "Begin simplifying your lifestyle before retirement. Unwind some of the complexities that you picked up along the way. Begin cleaning out, selling off, maybe even moving to simpler quarters. Get used to a more Spartan lifestyle before it hits." In reality, everything that we own owns us. So we are advised during the sunset season of ministry to maximize time with people by minimizing time on the maintenance of stuff.

Prepare for your last transition. George Bernard Shaw said it well: "The statistics on death are overwhelming, one out of every one dies." The greatest certainty of life is death. One motivating factor for living full and living well in our last season of life is the realization that we are finite people. Knowing that I am closer to the end of life makes the moments remaining more precious.

As pastors, we have walked with people through "the valley of the shadow of death" (Ps. 23:4). We know that some people have left their houses in order, but others have not. And although death is *homecoming* for the godly saint, we have witnessed the waves of grief that cascade on the loved ones who remain. Therefore, for the sake of our spouse and family, we need to ensure that the details of our final transition, our transition into glory, are in order.

Talking about final plans during the last weeks of life is difficult. Those moments are best reserved for reflecting on the good times shared together. Therefore, now is the time to make our spouse and children aware of our desires regarding life directives, funeral arrangements, favorite hymn or song, location of interment, and other physical details regarding our death. Our will should be current, and beneficiaries should be noted on all assets, such as titles, insurance policies, and certificates of deposit. A list of distribution of property should be maintained in a safety deposit box, the children even knowing ahead of time that such a list has been put together.

Once again, the point here is not to be overly morbid but succinctly to delineate how we want our *tent* taken care of when the real us goes to be with Christ. Then, with the details of our last moments planned, we are free to maximize our last season of ministry.

Enjoy the journey. Colleagues who have repositioned into part-time ministries or volunteer service have embraced a selectivity that ensures the most fulfillment. For example, one pastor agreed to work twenty hours a week in pastoral care. In this role, he was able to use his people skills but didn't have to hassle with staff meetings and other administrative functions that he disliked. Another minister negotiated an arrangement where he would work forty weeks per year, the weeks negotiable to accommodate trips that he and his wife desired to make.

Summary

At the repositioning stage of our lives we have *nothing to prove*. Although some pastors might have enjoyed all aspects of their ministerial journey, many pastors have acknowledged always feeling driven toward another destination. In this last season of ministry, we can now accept only those opportunities that we choose. We can limit engagements to only those activities that can make the greatest impact and offer the deepest fulfillment. We are now free to enjoy deeply our ministry journey.

EPILOGUE

My family is now in a life stage with four adult drivers. Each of us has his or her own car. Betsy zips around in a sporty sedan; Ben cruises in a *lifted* long-box truck; Barb enjoys "Madam Blueberry" (her Ford Contour); and I drive a small pickup. More important than the style in which we travel are the destinations of our journeys. Getting to the right place—whether it is work, church, a meeting, school, or a friend's house—is our primary concern.

Most of you reading this book already have a *license* to preach. Although some of you might prefer to serve a church in the Sunbelt or in New England, or one with a multiple staff and great facilities, serving in *the right place* is, no doubt, your primary concern. For this reason, times will arise when assessing ministry objectives is necessary.

Fortunately, as you approach intersections of transition, you are not alone. The Arranger of circumstance and Giver of peace provides sovereign guidance. Colleagues who have made the trip earlier have also shared their insights and counsel. By knowing yourselves and paying close attention to the directional signals, you can proceed with confidence on your ministry journey.

⋮ ENDNOTES

Chapter 4: Assessing Your Present Ministry: Personal Signals

1. The Personal Profile System, Inscape Publishing © 2001 St. Louis Park, Minn.
2. James D. Berkley, "What Are Pastors Paid?" *Leadership Journal* (spring 1992): 84–89.

Chapter 5: Assessing Your Present Ministry: Pastor/People Signals

1. *The Reader's Digest Great Encyclopedic Dictionary* (Pleasantville, N.Y.: Reader's Digest Associates, 1966), s.v. "signal."
2. Larry DeWitt, *Out of the Sanctuary and Into the Streets in the 90s* (Ventura, Calif.: Gospel Light Publications, 1989), cassette tape.
3. Mark Senter III, "Five Stages in Your Ministry Development," *Leadership Journal* (spring 1990): 90.
4. Oscar H. Reinboth, *Calls and Vacancies* (St. Louis: Concordia, 1967), 21.
5. J. W. Harbin, *When a Search Committee Comes . . . or Doesn't* (Nashville: Broadman, 1988), 55.

Chapter 6: Assessing an Invitation to Move: Congregational Signals

1. Haddon Robinson, *Expositapes* (Denver: Denver Seminary, 1983), 3:2.
2. Kenneth B. Bide and Allice M. Jones, *Yearbook of American and Canadian Churches* (Nashville: Abingdon Press, 1991), 278–83.

Chapter 7: Assessing an Invitation to Move: Personal Signals

1. Gerald Whiteman Gillespie, *The Restless Pastor* (Chicago: Moody, 1974), 21.
2. Larry Burkett, *The Financial Planning Workbook,* rev. ed. (Chicago: Moody, 1990), 29.

Chapter 9: Pastoral Assessment

1. Gene Getz, "Evaluating Personal Performance," in *Lenders,* ed. Harold Myra (Waco, Tex.: Word, 1987), 83.
2. Len Kageler, "Performance Reviews: Worth the Trouble?" *Leadership Journal* (summer 1985): 28.
3. Ibid., 27–28.
4. Robert G. Kemper, *What Every Church Member Should Know About Clergy* (New York: Pilgrim Press, 1985), 12.
5. Ibid., 13.
6. Getz, "Evaluating Personal Performance," 84.

Chapter 10: The Candidating Process

1. Kenneth Quick, "Candid Candidating," *Leadership Journal* (fall 1990): 72.
2. Ibid., 73.
3. David B. Biebel and Howard W. Lawrence, eds., *Pastors Are People Too* (Ventura, Calif.: Regal Books, 1986), 62.
4. Richard Nelson Bolles, "The Pastor's Parachute," *Leadership Journal* (summer 1990): 23.
5. Ibid., 23.
6. Dennis Newton Baker, "A Pastoral Search Manual for Conservative Baptist Association of Southern California" (D.Min. diss., Talbot School of Theology, 1992), 93.
7. Roy M. Oswald, *New Beginnings* (Washington, D.C.: Alban Institute, 1989), 26–27.

Chapter 11: Moving from Associate to Senior Pastor

1. *Innovate with C.A.R.E. Profile: Understanding and Valuing Your Contributions to Successful Innovative Teams* (Minneapolis: Inscape Publishing, 1995). Available through authorized distributors such as Ministry Transitions, Inc., www.ministrytransitions.org/profileinstruments.html.

Chapter 13: Moving from Congregation to Marketplace

1. John C. LaRue Jr., "Forced Exits: A Too-Common Ministry Hazard," *Your Church* (March–April 1996): 72.
2. See Elizabeth Kubler Ross, *On Death and Dying* (New York: Macmillan, 1969).

3. William Bridges, *Managing Transitions: Making the Most of Change.* (New York: Addison-Wesley Publishing Company, 1991), 37.
4. John C. LaRue Jr. "Forced Exits: Preparation and Survival," *Your Church* (July–August 1996): 64.

Chapter 14: When You Want to Move, but No One's Knocking

1. Richard Nelson Bolles, "The Pastor's Parachute," *Leadership Journal* (summer 1990): 22.
2. Andre Bustanoby, "Why Pastors Drop Out," *Christianity Today* (January 1977): 14.
3. Richard N. Bolles, "The Clergy Job Search: An Overview," in *Your Next Pastorate: Starting the Search,* ed. Richard N. Bolles, Russell C. Ayers, Arthur F. Miller, and Loren B. Mead (Washington, D.C.: Alban Institute, 1990), 2.
4. Arthur F. Miller Jr., "Build Your Search Around Your Giftedness," in *Your Next Pastorate: Starting the Search,* 8.
5. Bolles, "The Pastor's Parachute," 22.
6. Ibid., 24.
7. Bustanoby, "Why Pastors Drop Out," 15.
8. Rick Warren, *Leadership Network Compass* (spring 1992): 3.
9. *Pastor to Pastor* (Colorado Springs, Colo.: Focus on the Family). This bi-monthly cassette series features ministry interviews with church leaders, conducted by H. B. London. Available from 1-800-A-FAMILY.
10. *Audio-Tech Business Book Summaries.* Two cutting-edge business books are summarized each month. Available on cassette or CD at 1-800-776-1910.
11. Leadership Network provides conferences, resources, and several magazines. Call 1-800-765-5323, or visit www.leadnet.org.
12. Russell C. Ayers, "The Job Search: What Are My Choices?" in *Your Next Pastorate: Starting the Search,* 42.
13. Ibid., 36.
14. Myra Marshall, *Beyond Termination* (Nashville, Tenn.: Broadman Press, 1990), 151.

Chapter 15: Preparing the Church for a Pastoral Transition

1. Edward A. White, ed., *Saying Goodbye: A Time of Growth for Congregations and Pastors* (Washington, D.C.: Alban Institute, 1990), xi.
2. Donald Bubna, "How to Bid a Healthy Farewell," *Leadership Journal* (summer 1988): 120.
3. Ingram C. Pramley, "Reflections on Ending Ministry in a Congregation," in *Saying Goodbye,* 47.

Chapter 16: Jumping Out of the Blocks

1. Doug Scott, "Moving Right In," in *Transitions,* ed. Ed Bratcher, Robert Kemper, and Douglas Scott (Portland, Ore.: Multnomah, 1991), 63–64.
2. Katherine P. Cole, "Helping the Family Manage the Move," *Leadership Journal* (spring 1991): 81.
3. Margret B. Emerson and Katherine Cameron, *Moving: The Challenge of Change* (Nashville: Abingdon, 1988), 77.
4. Cole, "Helping the Family Manage the Move," 80.
5. Cheri Fuller, "Facing a New School," *Focus on the Family* (August 1991): 5.

Chapter 17: Retiring or Repositioning?

1. Ted W. Engstrom, *The Most Important Thing a Man Needs to Know About the Rest of His Life* (Old Tappan, N.J.: Revell, 1981), 107.
2. Ibid., 106.
3. Smiley Blanton, cited in Engstrom, *The Most Important Thing,* 107.
4. Jerry K. Robins, "Lessons in Retirement," *The Christian Sentry* (12 April 2000): 422.
5. Engstrom, *The Most Important Thing,* 109.
6. C. Van Elliot, CFP, Director of Financial Foundations, Big Bear Lake, California. Information given in an e-mail to the author. July 7, 2001.